W

We Will Be Heard:

A South African Exile Remembers

by

Bojana Vuyisile Jordan

QUINLAN PRESS
Boston

Published by:
Quinlan Press
131 Beverly Street
Boston, MA 02114

Library of Congress Cataloging-in-Publication Data

Jordan, Bojana Vuyisile, 1930-
  We will be heard.

  1. Jordan, Bojana Vuyisile, 1930-   . 2. Blacks--
South Africa--Biography. 3. South Africa--Race
relations. I. Title.
DT779.8.J63A3 1986   968.06'092'4 [B] 86-70325
ISBN 0-933341-43-1

Printed in the United States of America
August 1986

This book is dedicated to the memory of two illustrious men: my late uncle Archibald C. Mzolisa Jordan, my intellectual and social idol of all time, and Mangaliso Robert Sobukwe, my political and ideological mentor. My uncle showed me the necessity of merging the pursuit of knowledge and the creation of substance from that knowledge with the reality of living day to day with family and self. Sobukwe introduced ideals into my life towards which I shall always yearn and strive. I owe much of what I value in life to these two men, for whom I write:

Such a sleep they sleep,
The men I adored and admired so much.
Their souls will be happier
The day racist South Africa
Becomes a free Azania.

Contents

Maps ix

Preface 1

Introduction 3

1 A Lifeline in the Transkei 5

2 Life and Learning Beyond My Village 17

3 Traditional Life Between St. Johns and Lovedale 31

4 Lovedale Missionary Institute 49

5 Fort Hare University, Training Ground
    for Independence 67

6 *Yemk'imfundo,* or "Away Goes Education" 101

7 Capetown—A Lawyer Confronts the Law 129

8 Botswana, Temporary Home for an Exile 169

9 Zambia, Last Home in Africa 191

Footnotes 207

SOUTHERN AFRICA

ZAMBIA
(Northern Rhodesia)

ANGOLA
(Portuguese West Africa)

MALAWI
(Nyasaland)

Lusaka✳

Zomba✳

Kariba Lake

Victoria Falls

MOZAMBIQUE
(Portuguese East Africa)

Caprivri Strip

Salisbury✳

NAMIBIA
(South-West Africa)

ZIMBABWE
(Rhodesia)

BOTSWANA
(Bechuanaland)

Windhoek ✳

Kalahari Desert

✳Gaborone

Pretoria✳

Maputo

Mbabane✳

SWAZILAND

LESOTHO

Maseru✳

(Basutoland)

REPUBLIC OF
SOUTH AFRICA

SOUTH
ATLANTIC OCEAN

✳Cape Town

INDIAN OCEAN

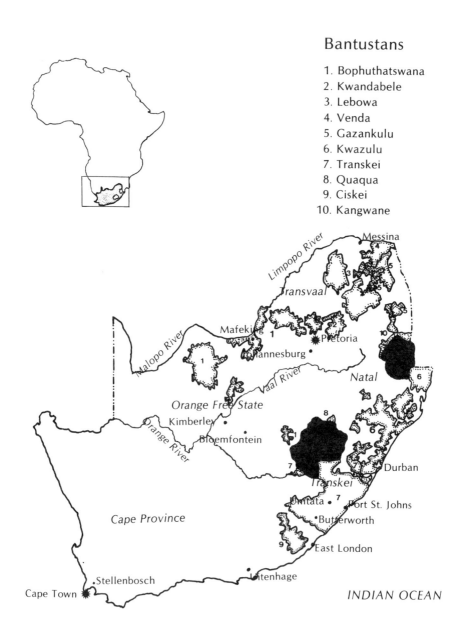

Bantustans

1. Bophuthatswana
2. Kwandabele
3. Lebowa
4. Venda
5. Gazankulu
6. Kwazulu
7. Transkei
8. Quaqua
9. Ciskei
10. Kangwane

Messina

Limpopo River

Transvaal

Mafeking

Johannesburg

Pretoria

Malopo River

Natal

Vaal River

Orange Free State

Kimberley

Bloemfontein

Orange River

Cape Province

Durban

Transkei

Umtata · Port St. Johns

·Butterworth

East London

·Stellenbosch

·Uitenhage

Cape Town

INDIAN OCEAN

SOUTH AFRICA

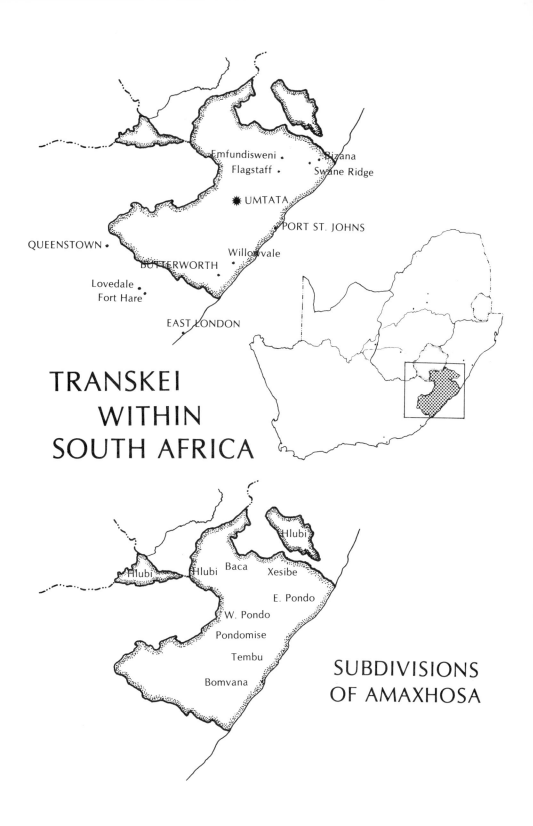

TRANSKEI
WITHIN
SOUTH AFRICA

Emfundisweni
Flagstaff
Bizana
Swane Ridge
UMTATA
PORT ST. JOHNS
QUEENSTOWN
Willowvale
BUTTERWORTH
Lovedale
Fort Hare
EAST LONDON

SUBDIVISIONS
OF AMAXHOSA

Hlubi
Hlubi
Hlubi
Baca
Xesibe
E. Pondo
W. Pondo
Pondomise
Tembu
Bomvana

Preface

Since the Nationalist Party came to power in 1948, many of South Africa's brightest and best-educated Africans have been lost to their people as they have either fled the country to escape the tyranny of the government or been silenced by imprisonment and brutalization.

We Will Be Heard is the autobiography of Boji Jordan, one of these bright young men who, against the severest of odds, reached upward from his rural origins to gain a university education. Eventually he began a career in law, only to be forced to flee South Africa in 1961 to avoid arrest for his efforts to organize African opposition against apartheid.

Jordan entered manhood in South Africa during the most dynamic period in the modern history of Africa and of his country. He began his education at Fort Hare University in 1950 when the continent was striving anew to break the chains of colonialism following the hiatus of World War II. Attending Fort Hare during that era were such luminaries of Africa's future as the late president of Botswana, Seretse Khama; the short-lived president of Uganda, Yusuf Lule; the current prime minister of Zimbabwe, Robert Mugabe; the founding president of the Pan-Africanist Congress, Robert Sobukwe; and Oliver Tambo, currently serving as acting president of the African National Congress.

In South Africa, as in the rest of Africa, the 1950s was an era of great hopes and dreams, culminating in the surge to independence for much of Africa. In South Africa, of course, the story was different. While 1960 is often described as the watershed year of African independence, for South Africa it was the year of the Sharpville-Langa massacres and the banning of the African National Congress and the Pan-Africanist Congress.

Jordan's sensitivity to the injustices in his country was to draw him increasingly into the struggle to ease the yoke of European oppression. It was his fate to be in Langa the bloody day of March 21, 1960, when Africans there and in Sharpville were killed in large numbers as they sought to meet the request of the Pan-Africanist Congress that all men go to the nearest police station to surrender their passbooks, which Jordan describes as "the most hated of all the symbols of oppression."

We Will Be Heard is infused with Jordan's love of the country of South Africa, with its beautiful vistas and its exciting potential, and his hatred of the white government and its ugly system of oppression. While the book is in part a polemic against that system, it is much more. It reveals how a person who can write with such love of his rural childhood, and who speaks of his willingness as a youth "to do anything to drink deeper of the quenching waters of knowledge," becomes a militant opponent of a system he describes as determined "to keep the African in perpetual, permanent servility and serfdom."

Finally, it is a story of both tragedy and hope, of a man forced to leave his country and people, the tap root of his being, but who continues to burn with the conviction that South Africa will gain its freedom as a transformed and vibrant Azania.

Dr. Thomas Nyquist

Dr. Nyquist, author of The African Middle Class Elite *and former president of the New York African Studies Association, is currently an administrator for the State University of New York Research Foundation.*

Introduction

When I came to Albany, New York, in 1981, I embarked on a new phase of my life. Although I had spent a lifetime fighting apartheid in Africa and then America, I had encountered periods of great discouragement and hardship, especially during my many years in the enormous frustrating cities of the United States. This was now to be a period of new beginnings, revived hope and meaningful activities.

My initial venture was to alert the people of Albany to the problems in South Africa by working with them in opposition to a South African rugby game scheduled to be played in the city. Within a year, I had made Albany my home. I had found helpful, generous people to assist in anti-apartheid work, and I was joined by partner-for-life in our personal love and public efforts for world-wide rights. In 1982 we organized the American South African Peoples' Friendship Association to promote good will among peoples and to bring an end to apartheid and racism.

As my friends and I engaged in many conversations and meetings about the monstrous system of apartheid, I was often queried about what it was really like to have lived in South Africa. Question after question pushed me further into my reflections on my life before I left Africa's shores. Born in the 1930s in the quiet green countryside of Swani Ridge in Pondoland, South Africa, where village mothers took turns helping my mother feed me, I never knew a local family without enough food or other items necessary for existence. There was enough milk to drink and to turn into "curdle" or a variety of other

3

foodstuffs. There were enough beehives for us boys to help ourselves to the honey, especially in summer. There were enough cattle to produce meat, which passed freely among the villagers. There was enough grain from the fields, plowed and tilled annually with spans of oxen. There were enough animal skins, tanned and made into beautiful clothing for the villagers.

As I grew to manhood, I saw the essential condiments of life—food, clothing, shelter—whittled away by the white man's laws. Education had been presented to us as a most necessary tool with which to swim the troubled waters of this world. We had accepted it seriously and had partaken of as much schooling as our parents' finances permitted. After years of high school and university education, I found myself forced by the white man's laws in the form of Bantu Education to unlearn what I had so fervently learned all my life. Even worse, as a teacher I was to indoctrinate others into believing that they were by nature inferior, that they were perpetually to be "hewers of wood and drawers of water." The Bantu Education Act was turning me into a tool of apartheid. Was I going to do what my conscience directed was the truth, or was I going to work for the white man and teach the way he wanted me to? Each man has to decide whether to be himself or to act in the image of some imposed ideology. I decided to be myself, and that is what this autobiography is all about.

The system of apartheid, appropriately called "a crime against humanity" by the United Nations and "twentieth-century slavery" by human rights organizations, has lit a fire of anger in me that can only be abated by a complete dismantling and destruction of that system. As I avidly read or hear every account of the quickening pace of black opposition and white governmental oppression in South Africa, I sense in part a replaying of the events that I experienced there. I remember the heroes at home whose advice and direction have gripped my soul. I had to write this book. I had to share my life and the lives of my compatriots with others so they would understand. In this way, we will be heard.

1

A Lifeline in the Transkei

I was born on June 19, 1930, the second of eight children, five boys and three girls, in the village of Swane Ridge in the Siphaqeni District of the Transkei, South Africa. My father was the principal of the village higher primary school and had met mother at the Emfundisweni Teacher Training School, where they both were students. Pending my birth, my grandmother came to live temporarily with my family when my mother was nine months' pregnant. By reason of experience and certification by the village elders in her own community of Emfundisweni, about twenty miles away, Grandma was a confirmed midwife. She had delivered my elder brother, Ntandazo, perfectly, and was only too happy to deliver me as well. Although there were a few other confirmed midwives in my village, it was cheaper to have Grandma, since the traditional fee of a few chickens, a goat or a sheep, depending on the wealth of the deliveree, would be waived in my mother's case. Besides that, Grandma would also help with the household chores, such as napkin cleaning and food preparation.

The story of my birth is typical of other babies in my village. Though Holy Cross Hospital was only about thirty miles away, less than 5 percent of the villagers were taken there to give birth; usually, only expectant mothers who had been very sick prior to delivery were taken to the hospital. It was far more desirable that the baby, especially a boy, be delivered at home so that any family customs could be administered immediately after birth. Some customs in my area applied to boys in particular, such as facial incisions in the case of the Pondo clan, or cutting the small finger in other Xhosa clans. Since I was of the Hlubi clan, something else had to be done to me after two days. Please do not ask what; it is a secret that I do not know and which my father, never having told me, took to his grave. I am curious to know about it myself. Whatever it was, it must have been special. I have no reason to complain of my early origins.

When my mother started feeling the pains of childbirth, her bed was removed from the bedroom she shared with my father to a small round *rondavel,* or dwelling, she would share with my grandmother. The bedstead was stored away temporarily, as it was customary that she deliver her baby on a mattress on the floor to be as close to Mother Earth as possible when bringing me into this world. I was delivered early on a Thursday morning, with only Grandma in attendance. There were no complications, so the other two village midwives who had volunteered to be around with their herbs in case they were needed were politely told they could go home. The only man allowed in shortly after my birth was the *ixhwele,* the family herbalist or doctor (whom some people mistakenly call a witch doctor), who dug a small hole three or four feet deep on the fireplace. There, my umbilical cord was buried and covered with corrugated iron. Afterwards, the fireplace was put to its regular use. This tradition is still followed to this day in some areas.

The same procedure was followed for the three brothers and three sisters who were born after me, each in a separate rondavel. Hence, apart from the three main houses at my old home in Swane Ridge, there are eight smaller buildings. Later, though our respective jobs and professions had scattered us all over South Africa, we occasionally had reunions, and it was with great pride that each of us pointed out the particular site where we were born. Some families in the Transkei still do gather—though not necessarily annually—as Americans do at Thanksgiving time. On these occasions there is usually a lot of feasting and entertainment. Meat, in particular, is always plentiful: usually an ox, some sheep and a few chickens will be slaughtered from the family livestock.

Because I was born a healthy baby by all accounts of the mid-wife, no one was allowed to see me until two days had passed. The exceptions, of course, were the ixhwele who had buried my umbilical cord and my father, who had only to see my face from the doorway to vouch that I was indeed his son. After a week my mother and I were strong enough to be joined by my father in our special abode. After two weeks we returned to the usual family bedroom used by my parents.

At this time a small feast was made for the next-door villagers and members of my family to welcome me into the community. Relatives brought a variety of dishes made from meat and corn which the women had cooked at home before setting out for the feast. People would finally see my face, and those who wished, such as aunts, could lift up and cajole me. Others brought presents of different kinds. My paternal uncle, Babana, who was a village cattle dip-tank supervisor, gave me a heifer that was expecting a calf. My mother, who is in her late seventies and now lives in the town of Mount Frere near Umtata, writes that there are still cattle from the lineage of that heifer in the family. I once boasted of owning no less than twenty cattle when I taught school in the Transkei in the fifties. My mother still keeps traces of my former possessions, not only for sentimental reasons, but because she knows that when I return, someone will have to account to me regarding them.

I am sure, at least, of what happened to one possession: to this day, somewhere in that abode where I was born in my beloved Transkei in Azania lies my umbilical cord. Whatever may since have happened to our former property, it is a village custom to allow me, whenever I want, to visit my umbilical cord. There lie my roots and my lifeline forever!

My Naming and Baptism

An especially significant event which occurred the day of my welcome-to-the-village feast was the announcement of my name. All the guests and family were well-fed and content. At this perfect time, my father announced the name given to me: Vuyisile Nelani. The latter name was taken from my great-grandfather. In his day, each person was given just one name, a name that was not held by another person and that had great

7

meaning to the individual and to the family. Nineteenth-century European imperialism was apparent to my forefathers, and the name Nelani was a message to the exploiters. It translates with difficulty into English as "You've had enough, be satisfied." Vuyisile means "Bringing happiness" or "Makes happy." Names were carefully selected by parents with the hope of lending purpose and direction to the life of each child. The naming was but one example of the recognition and appropriate treatment accorded each individual in Xhosa society.

I was still to be baptized by the Circuit Anglican Bishop, whose schedule would bring him to my village church school in about two months. The tradition was that I would be given a "Christian" name which would always be my first name. I was baptized Bransby Vuyisile Nelani Jordan by Bishop Bransby Key, who came from Holy Cross Anglican Mission.

All the children who were baptized in my village had to have some kind of English or Dutch name, referred to as "Christian," for the convenience of prospective and would-be masters and foreign white teachers. These names were given either by the parents or by missionaries or teachers who knew only white men's names. Those children who went to school without being baptized were given new first names at random by the village teachers. Many parents had never been to school or would not bother thinking of such names; some went to their own "churches" and worshiped their own ancestral gods.

The duty of giving Christian names, therefore, fell on my father during the registration of new pupils in his school, as it was an education department requirement of registration in our area. One of the arguments was that some African names were too long to fit within the columns of the register book. For instance, a friend of mine with whom I registered and who had been baptized or Christianized was called Zemkinkomomagwalandini Stata. The first name means "Away go the cattle, you cowards." His father had seen cattle being stolen by whites and hoped the name would be an incentive for his son to show no cowardice. This lad was renamed John Zemka. One boy's name was Mhlabamawahlulwe, meaning "Land must be divided." He was renamed Peter Mhlaba.

Most Xhosa names—Xhosa is my vernacular language—have specific meanings, and usually parents expect their children at least to live up to the connotation of their names. During my time this tendency of schools to change or add names was never popular with parents. Most of these Christian names had to be derived or borrowed from missionaries, shopkeepers or some other colonial settlers, or from politicians such as Cecil Rhodes, King George and General Smuts.

Many of my friends and colleagues have often asked why an undiluted African like me should have the last name Jordan, which is both English and foreign. I now hope to put to rest the notion that my parents liked to identify with the white man's names. In 1944 I had the privilege of asking my father about this strange surname. Other boys had been pestering me about it. Sometimes, when we were looking after cattle and roasting meat in the veld, there was not enough meat to go around. The older boys would use my last name as an excuse to sting me, saying, "There is not enough for descendants of white people."

According to my late father, Matthews Sigolani Jordan, the following account is how we unfortunately earned this surname. My grandfather, who was the first in the family to be baptized and Christianized, had the name Maqenukana. His other brothers were Siyongwana and Nobadula. Maqenukana worked for a farmer called Jordan. When he was baptized during the middle of the last century, the Anglican missionary who officiated had difficulty pronouncing the click "q" in Maqenukana and so, according to him, the name was a little too long for the church register. Since my grandfather worked for an Englishman called Jordan, and since he would have to cross the River Jordan before meeting the Lord, why not change the name to Jordan for the convenience of the priest, the former master and the Lord himself? My ancestor, good Christian that he was, readily agreed. After all, "a rose by any other name would smell as sweet." So let the world now know that my real surname is and should always have been Maqenukana.

All of this still does not account for my present nickname of Boji. To explain, I shall have to return to my babyhood. In that part of Africa, it was, and still is now, a usual practice to breast-feed African children from birth to at least three months. Most of the babies of my era were breast-fed for about six months, a diet supplemented by cow's milk and other tender foods.

In my case, it was a little different. I am told that I did not like either my mother's milk or cow's milk. When I was a month old, I would throw up at the very sight of my mother's breast. Both the white colonial doctor at Holy Cross Hospital and the ixhwele recommended that I be fed on African beer made of corn or millet, which seemed to agree very well with my system. Beer was brewed by every woman in the village on a rotation basis, and the men of the village would circulate throughout the different households where it was stored in *bojanas,* or pots, seven days a week. My mother was saved the trouble of brewing beer all the time just for me because when news spread in the village that *titshala,* or teacher, had a wonder boy who only drank beer, each day a different mother would come and pour some beer into my bojana. It soon became known in the village that it was so-and-so's day to visit bojana; hence, everybody in my village has called me Bojana for as long as I can remember. Boji is short for Bojana and is the name by which most English-speaking people address me. However, as you now know, it is only one name from several I have been assigned, be it Vuyisile Nelani, Bransby Jordan or the disregarded Maqenukana.

Early Schooling

Like all the other children, I went to the village school where my father was principal. Beginning at about six years of age, I would wake up at six in the morning with my older brother, milk the cows and the goats, and then drive them to the veld where older boys looked after them. Each of these older boys was remunerated for doing so with a heifer at the end of every six months, a common practice among cattle owners. One boy could look after the herds of as many as three to four families. At manhood, a boy who had thus cared for the cattle of others would often have twenty, thirty, even forty head of cattle.

Returning from the veld, we younger boys would wash up, have breakfast and walk to school at about 8:30.* The school was roughly three miles from home. My father, as the village

---

*Educationally speaking, the Transkei at this time was one of the more ad-

principal, was privileged to have a car, a 1925 Model T Ford which had to be started with a crankshaft. The only other car in the village belonged to the shopkeeper who lived down the road from the school. My father did not use the car often and only gave us rides to school on really cold days. Along the way he would pick up other kids, and by the time we reached school there would be about ten of us squeezed onto each other's laps. It was a lot of fun, and we used to look forward to cold days. When it rained hard, the road to school became very muddy and was not easy to traverse by car, so we walked as usual.

Fortunately, my home was about three hundred yards from the Bunga road. The local government of the Transkei, a region in the Cape Province, was called the Bunga. The Bunga had car-roads built for government or commercial enterprises. Big farmers were a distance from the villages, and private farmers built their own roads. There were very few bridges—only those leading to the government offices, which collected taxes and recruited labor, to shops, hospitals and stores. No roads went to the homes of the villagers. Most long-distance transportation by villagers was by horse. On rainy days, smaller kids who had to cross rivers were automatically excused from attending school. Big boys were expected to attend school and would be excused from carrying books. They would have to swim across some rivers, and though they would get to school wet, the school provided a fire in the fireplace of one classroom where they could dry their clothes. The maximum age was about thirteen or fourteen. It was nothing to stand naked among other boys; on the contrary, it was a lot of fun to see each other's private parts, big ones and small ones. Comments and jokes were good-naturedly exchanged.

---

vanced areas for blacks. Among children there, 40 percent of the total age group attended primary school. Most of these classes were co-educational. In secondary schools during the 1930s and 1940s, approximately 30 percent of the population of the appropriate age level attended classes. In both primary and secondary school, the male/female ratio was about 60/40. Girls were educated with the expectation that they would become teachers and nurses, but the major goal set by societal standards for females was marriage and motherhood. I cannot remember a single unmarried woman over twenty years old in my village. Once married, all women were excluded from teaching jobs.

All of primary education was a lot of fun for me, especially the higher I went in grade school. In addition, there was the joy of the delicious meals we were served after school at home. These consisted, in part, of corn, the use of which could be varied in different kinds of meals, such as *mngqusho, papa, marewu* and *mvubo* (milk, meat and different kinds of fruit). All of us looked forward to our sumptuous lunches. Most mothers worked in the cornfields until about noon, when they would go home to prepare afternoon meals for their families. The only exception would be on weekends, when boys would fend for lunch themselves in the grazing pastures. Mothers and daughters would collect all the dirty linen and clothes and carry it on their heads to be washed in the big rivers, normally quite a distance from the homes. Homes were built away from rivers because of regular floods in summer. In my area, it rains six to nine months out of the year. The region is sixty to seventy miles from the coastal region of the Indian Ocean, and the climate is generally Mediterranean. We saw frost only high up in the mountains, and even then it would hardly be over two inches for the entire winter (June to August).

I had good grades in primary school; in fact, I was an above-average student. I enjoyed sports very much, especially soccer and track events. Once every two months or so there would be competitions between school choirs that would last from early evening until the following morning. With great pleasure, we traveled on foot for ten to twenty miles to attend such concerts. We would start from our village in the late afternoon with the girls usually carrying food provisions for us. We did not carry food, as each boy had to be armed with two or three sticks in case boys from the villages through which we passed would want to molest the girls. We were their temporary guardians, *in loco parentis* since parents remained home and, more often than not, the teachers would follow later on horseback or crammed in my father's car. The car would take a very round-about route, as there were no direct car routes. We welcomed these long journeys because they gave us the opportunity to flirt with the girls—those of us who did not have steady girlfriends. Like most normal kids, I liked to make passes at girls. We enjoyed every minute—how I wish I could have stopped time there and then!

Normally, school was out at about 2:00 p.m. Later in the afternoon, we relieved the bigger boys who had been herding cattle during the daytime. This gave them a chance either to go hunting, to do odd jobs in the village like cultivating corn, or to go out looking for girls, either locally or in other villages. After milking the cows and getting the cattle in their *kraal*, or corral, we had supper. Then we settled down to homework by candlelight.

I used to look forward to herding cattle with the older boys, especially during the weekends. They would teach us younger boys a lot. In the early morning we took the cattle to graze in beautiful pastures, and in the early afternoon we took them to the river. In every pasture were our own quickly made mud-thatched huts for rainy or very cold days; these would be repaired thoroughly in the winter months, and periodically during the summer. In hot weather while the cattle rested under the trees, the bigger boys would teach us the art of swimming in those parts of the river that were not too deep. They would also show us how to fight with sticks. Stick-fighting was a necessary course in herdboyship because there were occasional confrontations with boys from other villages over the use of the best grazing pastures. The chiefs and the men of the villages left the determination of the use of pastures to the boys themselves.

On weekends, assignments would be decided early in the morning. One decision concerned who was to provide lunch for the day. A few boys were left to look after the communal herd of cattle. Others were assigned to hunt for wild cats, springboks, guinea fowls, rockrabbits and big birds; to dig up sweet potatoes; or to go for firewood, blueberries and mealie-cob. Some were assigned to steal peaches, plums, apples, grapes or whatever they could get from the adjoining farms, especially from the local shopkeeper's garden while he was busy selling groceries. I was usually assigned to the latter group. Before we went on this assignment we pledged never to tell on one another in case we were caught, although we were well-trained in the art of stealing. I was caught only once—at Mr. Rock's garden, stealing grapes. The local chief had me given five strokes with a light cane. I was in pain for a couple of days, and I made sure I was not caught again. Soon I was assigned to hunting. In the late afternoon we would then share all our booty: roast corn, roast meat and fruits. Now and again, we would tie the hind legs of some cows that were calving and drink the milk right from their udders. Calves were always left at home with the younger boys to look after them.

I certainly did not look forward to going to boarding school. Country life, in and out of school, provided all the fun of youth for me. I had plenty of friends and all the love I needed from my parents and from girls, either at school or on weekends from the bare-breasted ones who passed by us while fetching water from the rivers. There was plenty of food at home and at the cattle-grazing pastures. What more could a young boy want? I was a completely free human being, and life provided everything I needed. The land belonged to our parents and to us. The only contact with the white man was when the priest came to the church, when the inspector came to the school once a year or when I went shopping at the store, never more than twice a week. I was the color of the earth itself. As for those few strange white people, I hardly had occasion to be with them. They seemed to belong to a strange world, one with which I hardly had any real contact. Why worry about them when my land and its inhabitants offered me all I needed in life—my land, my home, my neighbors and their company?

Life is dynamic and never static; it has to keep on moving, just as the day follows the night. Technically, there is no present, merely a jumping thread from the past into the future. By the time I finish writing this one letter, it will not be this time but another time. This is what makes life so much fun. What may be bad at this moment you can determine to make good the next. I live my life the way I want to live it, and I want to make the best of it. I am not selfish, though; I know I must be my brother's keeper in whatever manner I consider best for both of our lives. One hand washes the other, just as we used to herd cattle—some boys providing firewood, others hunting, still others providing corn.

The African communal and social way of life—who has anything better than that? When I could not suckle my mother's

14

breast, the community, taking turns, provided me with beer. The life I lived as a youth must have been the universal umbilical cord to me from my ancestors' ancestors. I miss the green pastures and rivers of Africa. Little wonder, then, that Mangaliso Sobukwe, the founder/president of the Pan-Africanist Congress of Azania and all-time political mentor, wrote in 1959 in his inaugural address at the formation of the Congress: "Here is a tree rooted in African soil, nourished with waters from the rivers of Africa. Come and sit under its shade and become, with us, leaves of the same branch and branches of the same tree."

I miss those childhood years I spent in Pondoland, in the world that to me and my peers was perfect and unmolested by other men's greed. That was my home, and one way or another, I will struggle to renew those times in some shade, even though I know time moves and we must move with it. What is man-made can be man-unmade, because man is the most supreme animal on this earth.

2

Life and Learning Beyond My Village

The first taste of education my friends and I had only made us thirsty for more and willing to do anything to drink deeper of the quenching waters of knowledge. We certainly had not found anything repulsive in what we had experienced so far in our schooling, and the stories told to us by the older boys during their vacations from school enhanced our curiosity about the white man's ability to do so many wonderful things through education.

In our village the older boys who attended secondary boarding schools came home twice a year during winter and Christmas holidays, June and December, respectively. Their presence was incentive for us to attend Sunday school classes and the usual Sunday services. Churches were few and normally served a population of about ten squares miles. After services, the adults would have tea and bread, delicacies allowed to most of us only in the early mornings at home, and we would have corn bread and sugared hot water for tea. While we waited for parents or other elders to take us home, we gathered around the secondary school boys, who concentrated on narrating the good and glorious side of school life.

As youngsters we were captivated; we envied and hero-worshiped the boys for crossing rivers we had yet to see and for visiting white men's towns. We had heard all about Western civilization: how the boys dined with girls on Easter Sunday using forks and knives; how they learned about the history and geography of England and America; and how they learned the art of flying airplanes, a curiosity to us when they occasionally buzzed over our heads while we were in classes or herding cattle. When we first saw the airplanes flying like birds, we thought they were the same size as birds. The white man's ability to manipulate these vehicles was an achievement which inspired all of us to similar accomplishments.

We were told that the black American Joe Louis had become the world heavyweight boxing champion because, among other things, he had learned boxing skills from the Europeans with whom he had lived in America. We also learned that the great black leader Hannibal of North Africa had crossed the Alps on elephants and defeated the Romans. He had learned and developed his military skill and ingenuity from the white people with whom he had lived in North Africa. At that time, we didn't know that those "white people" were Arabs. What mattered to us was the proximity of North Africa to Europe. It occurred to us that the greater the European influence, the better everything was—or so we thought. We concluded that in order to be productive or progressive in life we had to be European-oriented.

In South Africa the emphasis on European culture, influence and "whiteness" is more pronounced than in any other place in the world. The enjoyment of all facilities in South Africa was, and still is, the prerogative of whites—in other words, strictly dependent on whether you are "European" or "non-European." Hence, there are signs in all public facilities marked "Europeans Only" or "Non-Europeans Only"; the latter, of course, is always of inferior status. This racism and discrimination has long existed in South Africa, from the day the first Europeans arrived at the Cape of Good Hope in 1652. Over the years it became more ensconced in the relationships between and among people of different skin color until, with the coming to power of the Afrikaner Nationalist Government in 1948, the racist system called "apartheid" became cemented into the legal system of the country.

Apartheid means "separateness" and specifically dictates that each group in South Africa—whites, Africans, Indians (from southern Asia) and coloreds (descendants of racially

18

mixed peoples)—is to remain separate from other groups. The purpose of this system is to keep whites in power over the other groups, especially over the African people who represent the overwhelming majority of the population. The British whites do not usually openly oppose apartheid, but in general comply with "the laws." Any white person from America, the Soviet Union, Norway, New Zealand, Canada, Argentina or anywhere else in the world is classsified as European in South Africa and therefore enjoys the "whites only" status. Even the Japanese and Chinese are regarded as Europeans, proving the point that human beings in South Africa are regarded in terms not only of their color but also in terms of their economic status. It does not matter that Japanese and Chinese are not "white"; their countries' economies graduate them into "European" status. Another group, the blacks of other countries who tour South Africa must carry an identification card describing them as "honorary whites" or "honorary Europeans."

Even after learning about apartheid, we believed as young teenagers that what we could not possibly achieve in our village as black youths, we could get through mastering the skills of education. We certainly did not see color as any impediment to higher learning. We could not change our color overnight in order to become white and privileged; instead, we believed we could utilize our brains to effect changes and improvements in man's way of life. Through education, we felt that we could reach any of the heights the white man had long monopolized and regarded as his sole domain. We were confident of our ability to conquer any odds and to overcome the barriers to success which society had placed in our way.

Most of the parents as well were eager for their children to have an education. Our parents expected school education to complement what a child learned at home, creating a truly pansophic development of the whole character and personality of the child. Education had to transcend the necessities of life and not merely consist of the three R's.

Parents sacrificed a lot to send their children to school. Education was neither free nor compulsory for blacks in South Africa, the opposite for Europeans in spite of the fact that Europeans were paid at least 50 percent more than Africans for all jobs. Even the poorest parent at the very least wanted his or her child to be able to read and write, and to learn more about manners. Education created a means of communication for wives with their beloved husbands, who spent three-quarters of their lives away from their families laboring for whites in mines, on farms or in urban areas. For their mothers, school children read letters from and wrote to fathers far away at work. Seventy-five percent of African mothers were and are "widows of the reserves." Today these women are the custodians and educators of their children in the arid and barren *bantustans*, or homelands, while the men live temporarily in the so-called "white" areas and labor in the mines and cities for slave wages.

I well remember the deferential treatment my father received in our village because he was the titshala. Once, when I was ten years old, my father and I were walking from the shop when we met a boy my age from another village. The average African child has awesome respect for his or her elders. Anyone of your mother or father's age is called "Father" or "Mother" so-and-so.

My father knew this boy's father, so after we had greeted him, my father asked the boy to convey his regards to his father. My father was not sure if the boy knew who he was, so he asked, "Who will you say sent greetings to your father?"

The boy answered, "I know your name, Father, but I cannot say it because at home we are taught not to call out older people's names."

My father responded, "All right, say it. It does not matter, your calling it out. I just wanted to make sure you knew it."

"You are Father Teacher." The poor boy, who himself was not attending school, was under the impression that "Teacher" was my father's surname.

Even though the advantages to be gained from education were obvious and my parents, like others, were in favor of further education for their children, I still felt a great deal of reluctance to go away to boarding school. Along with the good stories, the older boys had told us of the restrictions imposed upon them; their movements were limited to the boundaries of the school campus, they went out shopping about once a week and could socialize with the girls, who lived in separate dormitories, only on weekends.

In the village we did not have much trouble meeting girls. We usually walked with them to and from school. If there happened to be unfinished matters of love, we had a ready-made solution. Almost all the girls fetched water from rivers that were a distance from their homes. We knew where they lived and would often accompany them; however, when we neared their homes, we boys would turn back to avoid being seen by the parents, since the parents would feel the girls were being unnecessarily delayed in completing their work.

In these primary-school romances, when a boy and girl reached the point where they felt considerable affection for each other, the girl would cooperate in arranging a date even if the bucket was still full of water at home. When she knew the time the boy would be near the river, when she spotted him or when she heard the sound of his whistle, she would surreptitiously slip out and meet him by the river, emptying or spilling the water in the bucket so that they could have a reason to go to the river. It is hard to see outside a rondavel because most of these buildings have only two windows, so whistles, either handmade or from the mouth, were common dating signals. For instance, when I wanted to see my girlfriend Vuyelwa, I used to blow my whistle five times and she would be at a certain spot by the river, come rain or shine. I did not mind waiting for hours on end; I knew she would ultimately come. There is much improvisation in country life. I still love that life and treasure it above anything I now have. To this day, five is my lucky number.

There were other reasons for my reluctance to proceed to boarding school. I would also miss homemade foods. My mother was the queen of cooking as far as I was concerned. Her *mvubo* (fluffy cooked millet and sour cream) and *mngqusho* (beans with maize, gravy and seasonings) were mouth-watering even to think about. I knew I would even miss the food we prepared for ourselves during the weekends when we herded cattle. There was something special about the corn we roasted in deserted anthills in the summer. It was different from the cobs we had at home; it had a special smell and gravy-like taste. At boarding school we would use forks and knives. I had become so used to using my hands, and I so very much enjoyed licking my fingers, especially after a delicious meal of mutton or chicken made even more tasty by raw green pepper and sometimes leaves of certain trees known only to my mother.

Everything I had known and loved to that point was to be left behind for a while. My life had been circumscribed by village, school friends, other herdboys and family. The higher education for which I had been yearning sounded sweet at a distance, but parting from my surroundings was going to cause me much sadness. I would miss what had been part of me: the sounds of birds along the sweet running waters of the Swane River, the image of the setting sun on the ridges descending to the valleys and rising again, the aroma of flowers in the green pastures. I would miss the neighing of horses, the bellowing of cattle as we drove them back home from the pastures in the late afternoon, the bleating of sheep and goats, and even the barking of dogs at night. How much I would miss the skirmishes and stick fights that we had with the boys of the other villages—it was great when we were victorious and became heroes to the girls in our village! But even when we lost we would still have fun. Now, I was about to venture into a new world of education where my prowess had yet to be tried and proven. It is not so easy to part with the familiar.

But I convinced myself that all good things must come to an end temporarily. Education had to be worth more than the loss of these pleasures, I thought.

Secondary School* at St. John's

Early in the morning on the day of my departure, January 1945, I was ready to board the bus to St. Johns College on the

---

*Under the British educational system as it was established in South Africa, the titles of various levels of education differ from those in the United States. American grade school is always called "primary school" and consists of six grade levels. "Secondary school" is equivalent to American junior high school and consists of three years of education (Forms 1, 2 and 3). "High school" (Forms 4 and 5) is similar to American senior high school, but the final year is similar to the American first year at college.

outskirts of Umtata. St. Johns was an Anglican boys' boarding school run by missionaries and located about 200 miles from my home. My father could not drive me to the bus station as this was an ordinary school day and he had to teach school. My young brother Jongilizwe accompanied me on horseback to the Ntlenzi bus station. Two local girls who attended my primary school helped carry my suitcase and provision basket. I had been provided with the required school uniform, consisting of black blazer, white shirt, grey flannel trousers, and a black tie for Sundays, plus a couple of pairs of khaki pants and shirts for ordinary school days. My mother had filled the provision basket with a large chicken, a leg of mutton and a loaf of cornbread. She also had provided me with a bigger, empty basket which I was to fill with fruit collected along the way. I was given enough pocket money for incidentals such as soap and toothpaste to last about a month. I did not need any money along the route, as I had everything I really needed.

The bus left, heading for Port St. Johns, which was to be the major stop, about halfway to Umtata. Port St. Johns was a small port on the Indian Ocean between East London and Durban. Along the way we passed Gem Vale Mission, where the bus stopped so that we could pay homage to the grave of Bishop Bransby Key, who had been buried there some years back. I was glad and honored to kneel beside the grave of the man who had baptized me. About five miles from Port St. Johns, the scenery became astoundingly beautiful, with green vegetation and blooming flowers of all kinds along the way. The busdriver stopped twice to enable the few European passengers who were sitting in front to pick some flowers. Whites occupied the front of the bus; I don't remember at that age feeling upset or hostile about this.

The bus stopped in an alley about a hundred yards into the forest, and we were told we had half an hour to roam into the bushes and collect as much fruit as we wanted. As we moved into the wilds toward the sea, we could see scores and scores of trees, branches laden with peaches, apples, cherries and apricots. I filled my basket to the brim with the large, ripe fruits, as did the other boys. Each one of us collected enough fruit to last for a couple of weeks. Little wonder my mother had

23

provided me with that empty basket! During the winter (July) we would stop elsewhere, close to Port St. Johns, and fill our baskets with oranges and bananas. I still remember helping myself to those fruits with bees humming around, forming a bee-line to their hives. What a pity we could not help ourselves to their honey! I remember nests of beautiful birds, their singing filling the air around us.

Nature was so kind to us it seemed as if it were there to take the place of our parents. From my very first journey to school, my reluctance to leave the joys of home lessened because of the abundance of these fruits, provided by nature free of charge, a flickering of the bright and better life lying ahead of me in my education at Umtata. If the land of my birth could provide so much for me at no cost, it seemed reasonable to assume that education could provide even more.

I believe things have changed drastically since the forties and fifties in the area around St. Johns. It is now a "white spot" in the so-called bantustans.* The area where we used to collect all the fruit we wanted is now fenced in; you have to obtain a permit to go in and you have to pay for nature's bounty.

We enjoyed the bus trip to Umtata, as we were joined by other students, old and new, along the way. We reached the boarding school in the evening and were assigned dormitories, different dormitories for each grade group. About ten of us were assigned to ours, but fewer boys were in the upper-class dormitories.

On the following day we registered and then went to our respective classes. The school population was quite a cross-

---

*In 1976 the Transkei became the first of about a dozen bantustans, or "homelands," planned by the white racist government for South African blacks. The bantustans make up about 13 percent of the land in South Africa, which means 87 percent of the South African people are being given 13 percent of the land, land with dried-out, eroded soil where little water is available. The poor farming conditions that result lead to severe starvation and a high death rate among the people, forcing men to leave wives and children in the bantustans to look for work, another inhuman aspect of the apartheid policies. To make matters worse, bantustans are often a thousand kilometers away from cities, mines or other places where blacks might find employment. Many blacks enter the cities "illegally," according to apartheid, waiting to get a job and hoping to send money home to their families.

section of various ethnic groups, especially those representative of the Cape Province. The majority were Xhosa-speaking, with a sprinkling of Zulu- and Sotho-speaking. The social atmosphere was very friendly, and in the evening back at the dormitories, each boy would narrate stories about the way his family lived back home.

Our daily schedule started at 6:00 a.m. when we woke for showers. We had breakfast at 7:00 after a thirty-minute spree of manual work on the campus. Bells rang intermittently, reminding everyone of a change in chores or duties. Classes started at 8:00 each morning when we met for assembly. In good weather we met before the main offices; when weather was inclement we met in the big dining hall. The warden, Reverend J.W. Wilson, said the prayers, after which either or both of the principals (of the high school or the teacher training school) made announcements. Classes broke for lunch at 2:00 p.m. After lunch the boys were assigned different manual duties to perform from 3:00 to 5:00. From 5:00 to 6:00 was free-for-all time, which we utilized to get to know each other better. As the year went by, we discussed a variety of topics: starvation in one's particular area of origin; how to approach girls on Saturdays when we had permission to visit town; and of course, national affairs. Supper was served at 6:00, and from 7:00 to 9:00 we were back in the classrooms for evening studies. Lights were out in the dormitories from 10:00 p.m. until 6:00 a.m., when a new day began.

I found my classwork to be quite interesting and soon settled down to master it. There were two Junior Certificate Classes: A and B. Courses offered in the A class, which I attended, were English, Xhosa, mathematics, physical science, history, biology, and Latin. The B class offered all these courses except Latin and mathematics; instead, it offered physiology and hygiene. Our teachers were about 50 percent black and 50 percent white, with only two white women.

My two favorite teachers were Mr. Knowledge Guzana, who taught English, and Mr. Cadoc Mnqweno Kobus, who taught both history and mathematics. These two would digress from the given syllabus and introduce us to the politics of South Africa. Both were involved in what was happening in the community outside the classroom. Knowledge Guzana extolled the virtues of being learned and speaking "the King's language" flawlessly in order to be successful in future business circles. He was an excellent teacher, and we thought he spoke and taught English "as if he had been born in England."

Cadoc Mnqweno Kobus was another teacher of the highest order. How we wished he had been our history teacher instead of that white lady, Miss Beal! Once or so a week Teacher Kobus would digress from his algebra or geometry lesson and talk about our roles as black men. He used to impress upon us that we should have "black values": by this, he meant the whole purpose of pursuing an educational career should be to recover our land, which had been taken away by white men who had tricked us because we lacked education and could not fathom their tricks. "How could a whole ox be exchanged for an ordinary pocket knife, as Jan van Reibeeck and his white settlers used to do when they arrived at the Cape?" he would ask rhetorically.

Teacher Kobus would often disabuse us of the fallacy that we were the future leaders of our country. He would say, "Life is now, not tomorrow. You live it today and you have to change it now while you are still alive. Tomorrow may not see you. You may be dead. Change and improve everything now, today, while you can. Tomorrow will take care of itself."

Those words impressed me and left an everlasting imprint. I still subscribe to that philosophy. I have an inherent faith in the intrinsic good of man. Man is noble by nature and presumably strives constantly for that which is good for society itself. Anyone whom we find to be working against the goodness of nature itself must be sent reeling to the cemetery. That's the song of the good old folks who were real pragmatists.

Among the people who were visiting lecturers at St. Johns, the one whom I will remember forever is the present (1985) president of the bantustan of the Transkei, Kaiser D. Matanzima. An excellent teacher, he usually came once a week to teach a history class. At the time, he was an intern with the law firm of Hughes and Hughes in Umtata, and would lecture on the importance of studying and practicing law. The theme of one of his talks was that essentially it was a crime to be born black in the South African setting of the white-settler government.

There, most laws were designed to trap the black man, not to help him. Even if a black has committed no crime, he might be detained without rights until a charge against him could be fabricated. The black South African has no role in making the laws that judge him and condemn him. Only whites have the vote, free choice of job and residence, freedom of movement and the right to political expression. Now that Mantazima heads a local government, I hope he sees to it that the laws are made for the people, by the people.

We did not have evening classes on Fridays at St. Johns; instead, we held debates in one area, while seniors held debates elsewhere. For these debates, outside speakers were occasionally invited to address us on a variety of topics. Sometimes we listened to local and national politicians outlining the national situation in South Africa. Most of the time these speakers were black activists.

One who left a lasting impression on me was Govan Mbeki of the African National Congress. At the time, he was the general-secretary of the Transkei Organized Bodies, a federated body of progressive organizations engaged in mobilizing the people against general oppression. That was in 1945, before apartheid became written law. Apartheid became statutory law in 1948, when Dr. D.F. Malan was swept into power on the slogan of apartheid and white supremacy. Prior to this, repression of blacks had been intensive; apartheid merely legalized it and sealed any apparent loop-holes.*

Govan Mbeki had successfully mobilized the Africans in the Transkei to oppose the Rehabilitation Scheme, a project tied to a law which systematically forced the people to cull their cattle, limiting them to less than ten head per owner because the large numbers of cattle were "eroding the soil." The Rehabilitation Scheme even limited the acreage of land each family could till. The land taken by the government from the people was then

---

*White workers rallied behind Malan as they had under Herzog in 1936 when the United Party gained victory under the slogan, "White Workers Unite Against Blacks." At that time, the United Party formed a coalition with the then South African Labor Party.

declared vacant and allowed to lie barren. That same Govan Mbeki who inspired many of us is presently serving a life sentence for "high treason" in the notorious Robben Island Prison for political prisoners, one of the harshest and most despicable penitentiaries in the world.* It is called treason in South Africa to want your land back from the white racist settlers, or to want it ethically redistributed. That is the crime for which Govan Mbeki and thousands of others were sent to jail. He had already served twenty years of the life imprisonment sentence. Political prisoners in South Africa are not allowed remission of sentence as murderers and other criminals are allowed.

Some of the students at St. Johns College were law-abiding "good" boys, bookworms who let the outside world go on as usual. Some of us were quite eager to learn about the political and economic scene in South Africa—and the world. We wanted to follow through with the process of learning by making whatever contribution we could towards a better world for all. In the afternoons my group would discuss what we read in the newspapers in the school library. Some of these issues would also be discussed in our Friday debates, in the dormitories or along the banks of the Bilitsho River† after our manual labor in the evenings.

Our sole complaint directed toward the school concerned the quality of the food we were given. We kept sending delegations to protest and recommend improvements. When the authorities, who were predominately white, ignored our pleas, we decided to go on strike. After all, we paid for everything in

---

*For a complete description of the atrocities of this prison, see the book *Robben Island,* by Indres Naidoo as told to Albie Sachs, Vintage Books, 1983. Naidoo tells of the sordid, brutal racial cruelty which he both witnessed and was subjected to as a victim of political oppression in South Africa. He vividly describes the agony, torment and torture inflicted upon the political prisoners under conditions equaled only in the Nazi concentration camps.

†Bilitsho was the river to the west of Umtata which separated that side of the school from Ncambedlana, a typical village and not part of the campus.

that school, not only the food but also books, services and upkeep. Our plan of action was to attack, with sticks and stones, all official signs of authority, including the residences and offices of the boarding master, the warden, the prefect and some of the staff members who did not sympathize with us when we raised the issue in classes. We were intent on storming and bombing the Bastille. The strike was staged on an October evening in 1946. The authorities called the police.

When the police arrived, they promptly sprayed tear gas on all of us. This was my first experience with the effects of tear gas. It was a terrible ordeal; the gas gets into your eyes, and you cannot see properly. Tears begin to flow, you suffocate and cough. Your legs feel weak, then wobble and shake. When the police clubbed us with their batons, we started falling on top of each other. We were totally subdued. The police were able to drive us as a group onto the football grounds, where they had us sit while they sprayed some more tear gas. Then, they left us there while they went around the school collecting those who had either gone back to the dormitories to hide under the beds or those who were trying to escape by crossing the Umtata River. By early morning they had rounded up the entire school population onto the football field.

At sunrise the police marched us through the town to the police station, where we were to be finger-printed and charged with public violence. We marched through the town four-abreast, singing a very common hymn at school—the words seemed to fit the occasion:

> *Onward, Christian soldiers,*
> *Marching as to war,*
> *With the Cross of Jesus,*
> *Going on before!*

We had a lot of fun waking up the townspeople, who peeped through their doors and windows at us.

Some of us gave fictitious names to the authorities. I was Accused Number 144, and I gave as my first name "Mfenemazabiwe," meaning, "Baboons must be distributed equally." We were not locked up and were allowed to go back to school after paying bail of five pounds each. Friends and relatives paid the bail for most of us. Mine was paid by my uncle Roro, who worked for the Bunga.

The case was tried for a week. It was still fun for some of us. We kept on interrupting and howling at the state, or crown, witnesses: the school prefects, the boarding master and the principal. Occasionally we would shout in unison, "Liars! Sell-outs!" When asked who made the remark, everybody replied, "Not me." We were all found guilty. Those sixteen years old and younger got five strokes with a light cane, those sixteen to eighteen got ten strokes, and those over eighteen (there were about ten of them) were fined ten pounds or one month in jail. Parents and friends of the family paid the fines for them.

We were all allowed back in school to continue with our studies. In November we wrote our final examinations. I passed the Junior Certificate in the first grade with an A mark and was even awarded a Bunga scholarship to continue with my high school education.

The end of the school year came in December, and we returned to our respective homes. The following year, 1948, I was to continue with my high school education at a different school: Lovedale Missionary Institute in the Ciskeian Region of the Cape Province. St. Johns College had both a high school and a teacher training school, so I could have finished all my pre-university education there; however, my father and uncles all had at one time or another attended school at Lovedale Institute, which was considered to be a prestigious school, and my parents felt that I had to follow the family tradition, especially since I had received such good grades in my junior secondary education.

Before going to Lovedale, I was to become a man. As soon as I returned home from junior secondary school, arrangements were made for that once-in-a-lifetime ceremony: circumcision.

3

Traditional Life Between St. Johns and Lovedale

When I was growing up in my beloved village of Swani Ridge, the elders emphasized that there were four extremely significant events marking stages in every man's life: birth, circumcision/initiation, marriage and death. My education would never be pansophic—intellectually, physically and morally complete in the development of body, soul and national consciousness—without the traditional initiation via circumcision into the world of manhood.

Of all the stages I was to go through in preparing myself to be a productive member of my society and community, the ritual of circumcision captivated my curiosity and aroused my anxiety the most. After all, I had experienced birth and felt that I simply was not even present during the event. Somebody else experienced it for me, and later I was only too happy to be around, joining the chorus of boys and girls already in existence. As for formal education, I had already tasted quite a bit, and it was a most welcome part of me. I always thought education was something I could not do without. Circumcision was equally important.

I was filled with curiosity about circumcision, but among the AmaXhosa it is a closely guarded custom. You have to have been part of the ritual to know anything about it. I begged my father several times to brief me, but to no avail. I even quoted to him his favorite African idiom— "Not to know is bad; not to wish to know is worse"—to convince him of the necessity of my knowing at least the rituals involved. His polite, teacher-like answer was always "Son, some things in life have to be experienced to be known. After all, most knowledge derives from some kind of new experience of pioneers. Wait until you get to the traditional school of circumcision to be all knowledgeable about it. You will have a teacher there whose sole profession is to lecture you on the ritual itself." I could not persist, since I knew that my day would come to be honored. Besides, there are certain limits to your discussions with elders; by African custom, you are not permitted to ask too many questions.

Circumcision is practiced by all except a small minority of Xhosa-speaking people, and there are virtually no deviations from the societal standards of acceptance of this ritual. Circumcision lodges are found all over the Xhosa-speaking regions, and within these areas there are only very minor variations in the practical procedures. When I was at secondary school, certain privileges were denied us as non-circumcised boys within the school precincts. For instance, we had to wait until those who were circumcised had finished before we had our baths and showers. When any of the already circumcised young men demanded that we wash their spoons after meals, or quickly polish their shoes on Sundays, we did it without question. Since they were our seniors by manhood tradition, we had to obey them without a word.

Every three or four years, boys were circumcised at puberty in rather large groups. I was seventeen years old at the time of my circumcision. The younger you are, the better your chances of healing quickly. Fathers with eligible sons would apply to their chief to build a lodge in a chosen area. After the chief made the arrangements for the plot of land, the fathers collectively built the lodge; some cleared the land, some did the thatching, some collected wood. Like many affairs, this was a communal undertaking. The lodge was usually a dome-shaped hut, the size depending on the number of youths to be housed.

Usually the ritual was performed in winter. Wounds heal more quickly out in the open in winter than in summer. Another factor favoring wintertime was the absence of storms, a reassurance against the likelihood of the lodge being struck by lightning. Although such a tragedy could be viewed as a natural phenomenon, those who were superstitious would believe it was the result of supernatural intervention by someone who held a grudge against one of the initiates.

Soon after my arrival home for Christmas holidays in 1947, it was arranged for me to join about ten of my peers for circumcision somewhere up in the mountains, away from the villages and people. My group obtained special dispensation from the chief and the lodge overseer to be circumcised in summer because we were all secondary and high school students who had just finished the school year. The school year in most African countries runs from January to December, and Christmas holidays were our longest stretch away from school. As we were to be initiated for at least two months, this seemed to be the best time for my group. Permission had been obtained from Lovedale authorities for me to arrive back at school in late January or early February.

Another advantage to my being circumcised soon after completing my Junior Certificate at St. Johns College was that, after circumcision, all the clothing I used as a boy was either to be discarded or given to my younger brothers because I had to literally throw away my past as a boy to enter into a completely new life of manhood, spiritually, emotionally and physically. A new or different wardrobe was an outward manifestation of this, so it was economically sound that I enter high school no more as a boy, but as a man, with new clothes and a new uniform for a different school.

The man selected as *khankatha,* or overseer, to the lodge ordered our fathers to report with us on a specified day. My father left me at the lodge with the other youths. We were ushered into a sheep pen, where our heads were shaved and our clothes removed by a small circle of solicitous male friends and relatives, some young, some old, but all circumcised. The circumcision was performed by an *ingcibi,* or medicine man, reknowned for his dexterity with an *assegai* blade. I was ordered by the ingcibi to say four words after him: "I am a man." After those words the surgical operation of removing the foreskin from my penis was over in a matter of seconds. I can only remember the thud and slash of the shining spear. I was not given any injection or anesthesia to counter the pain, but believe me, I felt no pain whatsoever at the time—it came later! The good old uncle who peformed this operation was as capable as any Western surgeon. I was not supposed to sigh, moan or clench a fist, twitch a toe, frown or even blink. I was brave, for in a circumcision lodge a coward is spurned by his fellow initiates and ridiculed by visitors. Seldom are there signs of cowardice in any way among the initiates; that would bring embarrassment and shame to your father, and you would be reprimanded and despised by your peers for many years to come.

From the moment we were circumcised to the day we left the lodge some two-and-a-half months later, we were subjected to much hardship. My loins ached and my body was stiff from turning on crude bedsteads made from branches and bamboo staves. We were aroused each morning at dawn to attend to our festering wounds at the edge of a nearby stream. We gently washed and dressed them with the soft, porous leaves of a local shrub and wrapped them in the silken sheaths of a large, onion-like bulb. Our bodies were also daubed with white clay as a purificatory measure. For about two weeks, while the wounds were healing, we remained confined to the lodge. We were draped in white blankets or sheepskin *karosses* and given menial jobs by the khankatha.

We spent hours basking in the sun, where we would sit talking in whispers about our pains, confiding in each other our cravings for self-rolled cigarettes, a pinch of snuff or draught of beer, and telling how we missed our girlfriends. We longed for homemade food, since our meals consisted of last year's corn-on-the-cob, sometimes burnt hard like river pebbles. To drink we had almost nothing except water, thickened by mud-like clay, but since the most painful thing to do was to urinate, the less we drank of anything, the less we would be involved in that torturous process.

Those first two weeks were hard to bear, and we all became withdrawn, subdued and docile. However frivolous, irresponsible or delinquent a boy may have been before circumcision, once he was broken down and taught to bow to the rigid codes of the lodge, he was sure to emerge as a sober-minded, respectable adult. The rules and restrictions of a lodge are manifold, and punishment follows swiftly upon all acts of transgression, however trivial. Even the most mundane conversation can lead to trouble, for the lodge has a secret jargon of its own which, if not correctly used by the initiates, earns them a whipping. For example, words such as hut, door, bed, mat, fire, dog and sheep-pen are replaced by exotic terms. Upon realization of the consequences should a slip be made, mind and tongue worked together in perfect unison and with flawless precision. Time passed slowly in that lodge, but because we had been taught since childhood that pain is cured by pain itself, we showed no signs of impatience. Another tenet we were taught was "That which cannot be cured must be endured." Sometime during the second week our wounds became itchy; this meant that the thorniest part of the journey had been left behind. We were then in a position to smile a little bit.

Later we were sent out by the khankatha into the surrounding hills, valleys and woods to search for food, as tradition dictates that a man must know how to fend for himself, even if it means stealing from outlying homes. When this second stage of our ordeal arrived, we left the lodge in twos or threes, our blankets and karosses matching the white of our clay-daubed bodies. Armed with sticks, spears and battle-axes and accompanied by fleet-footed, whippet-like dogs, we set out to hunt for birds, hares and even domestic fowl which would stray from some homes. We pilfered granaries, robbed eggs and stole meat hung out to dry by some household patriarch. There were limits, however, to this encouraged adventure into theft. Should we be caught red-handed, we would be thrashed first by the captor and then later at the lodge by the khankatha.

After about a month, this period of roaming, hunting and stealing came to an end. We then spent most of our time back in the lodge where, among other things, we were taught the delicate steps of an ancient dance. This khwetha dance, or dance of the initiates, forms part of the ceremony at the closing of the lodge, that longed-for day when we would be presented to relatives and friends as full-fledged adult men. When we emerged from the initiation lodge, humbled by the ordeal of circumcision and sobered by almost three months of hardship, we no longer would have thoughts for trivial matters. At least *I* had no trivial thoughts, and hopefully I have not indulged in many since then.

On the morning of the final day in the lodge, we rose at cock-crow and started the lengthy task of decorating torsos and limbs with exotic designs. With clays (mainly yellow and red), soot, ash and "washing-blue" cubes, we drew circles, ovals, squares and triangles, all intertwined with straight, curly or zigzag stripes. These patterns stood out wildly against the background of bodies that had been daubed white since the day of circumcision. At mid-morning we put on our khwetha regalia. This included masks, lofty headdresses and voluminous, ballerina-like skirts of palm fronds.

Meanwhile, a noisy crowd had been gathering in the immediate vicinity of the lodge: blanketed and turbaned relatives, friends and acquaintances, and women and maidens bearing gifts. When eventually we appeared, lining up shoulder to shoulder to begin the kwetha dance, we were greeted with cheering, whistling and the clatter of fighting sticks. Close by, a group of elderly women took up positions around an ox hide strung across a circle of upright poles. Singing a kwetha song, the women beat out its rhythm with sticks, pausing from time to time to take a pinch of snuff or to enjoy a mug of African beer.

Up we came, with a half-dancing, half-prancing rhythmic movement—not much stamping of feet, no leaping or writhing or turning about. With our bodies erect and arms gracefully at our sides, we did no more than jerkily raise and drop our heels in time to the singing and drumming. To add to the rhythm, the spectators joined in clapping their hands and smacking their fighting sticks together.

We must have been at it for at least an hour when the khankatha brought the dance to a close. We then ran off to the lodge and quickly stripped, tossing our regalia onto a pile, followed by everything else we had used during the past few months. Next we ran down to the nearby stream. Plunging into the water, we washed the white from our bodies, removing every trace of the clay that had covered our skins since the day of circumcision. Thoroughly cleaned, we redaubed ourselves with clay, this time of the red variety which symbolized our return to the community as men.

Meanwhile, the lodge was set alight. Although our nostrils were filled with the smell of smoke and our ears with the crackle of the flames, we dared not look at the fire in order to avoid misfortune in the years ahead. When the lodge was completely burned down, we were escorted from the stream back to the place where the crowd awaited us. Still naked, we hid ourselves behind a herd of cattle. When we reached the vicinity of the smoldering lodge, we were given new blankets to wear, some freshly dyed with red ocher.

We were then welcomed by relatives, sweethearts and friends, extolled as heroes, hailed as adults eligible for marriage and parenthood, and showered with gifts of all kinds. Best of all, we were showered with love. The rest of the day we joined in the feasting and dancing arranged to celebrate our return to everyday community life.

A succession of speeches followed, delivered by fathers who had been selected by the elders; these were lengthy discourses on Xhosa customs, behavior and etiquette, on the host of responsibilities we would have to face and on the high standard of behavior expected of us. I still remember that sultry Saturday afternoon in February 1948—those speeches lasted no less than four hours! Towards the end, thunderclouds appeared on the horizon and there was every sign that a fierce storm would burst before nightfall. Fortunately, since February was usually one of the wettest months, our guests had carried umbrellas, raincoats and hats and had even prepared shelters for the food and cooking utensils. Sure enough, as the sun began to slope toward the hills, the clouds quickly gathered, and in a very short time the sky was enveloped by an enormous blanket. Blinding flashes of lightning split the sky, thunder roared and fierce rain lashed the earth. Everybody ran into the nearest rondavel. The major concern was for the food, meats and delicacies that had been cooked previously and abandoned in the pursuit of cover. The roofs of some rondavels were blown away, and trees were uprooted from the earth.

As soon as the storm was over, we all came out, shook hands with old friends and hugged our sweethearts. The belief was held that all those graduates from circumcision that day would be rich men—since rain meant so much for food crops, it also would mean success for our lives. I am still looking forward to the fulfillment of that promise: going back to the land of my birth to till the soil and produce enough crops to feed my countrypeople, the promise that was made by nature itself on the day of my graduation from circumcision.

Circumcision is a highly respected ceremony among the AmaXhosa. Until the end of the eighteenth century, circumcision formed part of the puberty rites of all major South African tribes. After 1816, however, the practice was abolished by King Tshaka in all territories overrun by his Zulu armies. Determined to mold the motley tribes and clans into a homogeneous nation, he needed every available youth for his fighting forces, so he closed down the circumcision lodges upon conquering a territory and had the initiates brought to his military camps to become loyal to him and to his goals. His nets were cast as far south as the Mzimvubu River, isolating the AmaMpondo (who lived in the region from the Mzimvubu River north to the Mzimkulu River) from the rest of their Xhosa grouping to the south of the Mzimvubu River. Thus, to this day the great majority of the AmaXhosa south of Mzimvubu continue to practice circumcision and look askance at their uncircumcised brethren to the north of the river. So it is because of the ravages of the armies of Tshaka that the AmaMpondo of eastern Pondoland abandoned circumcision. I grew up in Pondoland, but since my father was of the Hlubi clan and a teacher—many teachers, ministers and governmental employees arranged for circumcision for their sons even while living in non-circumcision areas—I was circumcised.

One additional, curious lack of circumcision in this region needs to be mentioned. Considering that only Eastern Pondoland was overrun by the armies of Tshaka, there was no need for the youth of Pondoland West to be drafted into Tshaka's army, so there had to be a different reason for their abandoning the ritual. Besides, the people of Western Pondoland, the AmaMpondo, were and still are so close to the Bomvana, Tembu and Mpondomise people (also subgroupings or clans of the Xhosa) both geographically and culturally that it would take a catastrophic event for them to no longer observe a lauded custom like circumcision. The latter three ethnic groups still observe the circumcision ritual to the letter.

Mlengana Mountain in the Libode District held the key to this puzzle and was a frightening memory for all those of my age group who knew the story. This mountain is a gigantic mass of rock resembling a huge sugar loaf, with a face as vertical as a plumb line. So attractive and challenging is its powerful presence that practically all the drivers of our buses en route to school would stop underneath it so that we could take a closer look. Most tourists who visit the Transkei usually take the time to observe its beauty and splendor. Mlengana Rock, or Execution Rock, as it is popularly known, is situated approximately halfway between Umtata and Port St. Johns. Its summit is very difficult to reach, so the name Execution Rock, which is supplanting Mlengana Rock, seems to be a misnomer. It is doubtful that the peaceloving people of this area would have dragged a miscreant all the way to the top for the dubious pleasure of throwing him over. Rather, the story linking this mountain to the ritual of circumcision is a more plausible reason for its name to those who know Xhosa customs.

Legend has it that in the later stages of their initiation, the young Pondo men would transfer their circumcision lodge to the top of the mountain. The climbing of the rock with the material to erect a lodge was part of the initiation process itself during the middle of the last century; it was the kind of hardship that the young men would need to endure to be prepared to face their future lives. Furthermore, the top of the mountain was an ideal spot for the initiates to bask in the winter sunshine while recovering from their wounds.

The last group of initiates on the mountain were trapped in a fire in their lodge. To this day, the origins of the fire are the subject of superstitious speculation. One rumor circulated over the ages was that some jealous clans hired a medicine man to cause the fire in the lodge, either through an *impundulu,* or lightning bird,* or through some other magic. Whatever the truth may be

---

*This refers to the force or spirit within the natural phenomenon of lightning. The AmaXhosa believe that the spirits within nature can influence and manipulate happenings.

about its origin, all the initiates died either in the fire or while jumping over the rock as they ran away from the fire which engulfed the entire top of the mountain. This was such a tragedy for the community that the king of Western Pondoland decreed that circumcision be banned.

In most of the Transkei, boys were afforded the opportunity to become young men, to pass from social immaturity to maturity, in a meaningful way by the rite of circumcision. I will always remember my graduation from boyhood to manhood. The basic theme of the graduation speeches was that we were henceforth to live for the betterment of ourselves, our families and the whole nation. I was convinced by the elders on this day of graduation that I would always belong to the nation and continent of Africa, and that whatever I would do would be for the good of Africa. This has been the test of manhood in my life and in that of my peers in South Africa.

In Search of a Diviner

When I returned home from the initiation school, one of the leading elders of the village was seriously ill. An urgent meeting of the men of the village was held to inquire into the causes of the man's sickness. It was resolved that a group of six men should go to a faraway territory and find out from the diviners what the illness was about and who or what had caused it. It was also decided that I, as a newly graduated young man, should join the delegation so I could learn something about witchcraft. In traditional societies it was customary to give a young man "of promise" some experience in community affairs; he, in turn, would report to his peers what had taken place.

I was inwardly delighted to have been chosen—it was not considered proper to show my feelings about the selection—as I had always been extremely curious about witchcraft and divination. Almost all of my family and kin had been greatly influenced by the European institutions of church and school; therefore, they had neither told nor exposed me to many traditional beliefs regarding supernatural powers. I hoped this trip would answer some of the questions in my mind. I already had heard about witches, diviners, priests, sorcerers and prophets, viewed in African societies as persons with superior insight. When trouble or disaster affected an individual or society, these people were somehow involved. I knew little about the details, so this was going to be a real learning experience for me.

The day after the village meeting we left and headed toward Zululand, north into Natal. In Pondoland the Zulu people were respected as experts in divination. We set out on horseback with no particular destination in mind; this would be determined by the first diviner or witch doctor we encountered, who would convince us that he or she knew why we were traveling and what we were seeking. According to custom among the AmaXhosa, the diviner would know about our mission without our telling him or her and then would explain it to us and suggest solutions to the sickness.

At sunset on the first day, we stopped at a home in the Bizana area and asked to be accommodated for the night. We had looked for a large homestead which we could assume would have no difficulty in housing us. In the old African societies, people would never turn strangers away but would always welcome them with pleasure and make provision for them. We were fed, and before we retired for the night, the leader of our party explained the purpose of our journey and inquired from our host if he knew anyone who could be of help to us. He replied that he had an idea of the area across the Mtamvuna River where such experts could be found, and the following day we resumed our journey at his instruction. We passed by a shop in the Nomlacu area where we bought some bread, jam and cold drinks, and then continued our travels.

By late afternoon, when the shadows of the hills of Nomlacu had lengthened and touched the valleys below, we came to a halt in the *nkundla,* or foyer, of an imposing homestead overlooking the waters of the Mtamvuna River. The previous night's host had recommended this stop to us. We dismounted and introduced ourselves to the owner of the home, a gray-haired old man with a dark brown complexion who wore a bright red blanket. He must have been an impressive figure in his day, for he was tall and still carried himself well. He had a sharp eye and a deep expression which suggested quick intelligence. He was kind to us and told us to unsaddle our horses. Because of the warmth of the summer's day, those horses with light brown coats had turned a speckled brown, while the gray horses had become dun-gray with sweat. When they were relieved of their saddles, each steed bent its neck and cropped the grass, now rolling and tossing and tumbling, now straddling and urinating, now giving a long, drawn-out snort.

As we sat on the green grass near the cattle kraal, the old man was joined by two other elders. Conversation ensued among the elders; they inquired about each other's health and the health of their loved ones and explained about the droughts, taxes, epidemics of whooping cough and other calamities in their different areas.

A most interesting conversation then commenced. The old man, whose name was Dunga, turned to me. "Seems you are a school boy, Son, aren't you?"

"Yes, Father, I am. I just completed Junior Certificate at Umtata."

"Very well, Son," he said. "You see, we will only consider your education complete if you go to Lovedale after Umtata." He continued. "We of the Royal Readers* feel that only Lovedale can provide a well-rounded education, both culturally and intellectually."

For hundreds of years much learning, including history, was passed from generation to generation during evening conversations or storytelling.† These oral recountings of historical tales were regarded as essential for the orientation and adaptation of the individual to society. Thoughts about the past provided background for correct views of the present and afforded a clearer perspective on the future. Also, it was a great communal activity in which everyone could join.

One of our host's colleagues asked if I had been taught at Umtata how Pondoland was annexed by the white man in 1894. He

---

*The Royal Readers were the first English grammar books which taught the rudiments of the King's English, English "at its best." The people who learned from these spoke flawless English, "through the nose," as the saying went, meaning a good imitation of an English accent.

†It is sad to say that in the urban slums of South Africa, people are not free to assemble—permits are required to hold meetings—and so the oral literary and historical traditions have almost disappeared.

referred to the annexation of the Pondoland Tribal Independent State to the Cape Colony, South Africa, which was controlled at the time by the British government in England and Cape Town. The truth was, I had not been told about it in the three years in which I studied history at Umtata, so he told me his version, which he emphasized was an unwritten history because the whites were ashamed of the way they had induced Sigcau, the Pondo king, to sign papers of annexation.

The oral account of how Pondoland was annexed at the point of a gun by the British was narrated as follows: "By the end of the nineteenth century, all of the Cape Province, except for Pondoland, had been colonized by the British and was flying the British flag to show their rule. The British governor, Sir Henry Elliott, had come to Umtata to negotiate the annexation of Pondoland to the rest of the Cape Province. Most of the Xhosa-speaking peoples, except for those in Pondoland, had either allowed their territory to be colonized after being defeated on the battlefield or had just surrendered before the might of the British guns. They had practically no guns to fight back; all their resistance had been with spears.

"Sir Henry Elliott arranged a meeting with the Pondo king, Sigcau, and his counselors just outside Umtata, across the Umtata River at Ncambedlana Village. There Elliott arranged that some fat oxen be brought within sight of the meeting with the king. The Pondo king and his men relaxed when they saw the oxen driven toward them; it was customary that any stranger, especially a foreigner, should bring gifts when he interviewed the king. They naturally thought these oxen were gifts or were to be slaughtered in honor of the king. The oxen were going to be killed in front of the king, but not for him, nor for his honor.

"After speaking with the king and his men, trying to convince them that they should submit to British rule and become Her Majesty's subjects, Henry Elliott found that the Pondo king could not be moved one inch towards accepting that his land be ruled by anyone other than himself. He then decided to devise some other 'bloodless' tactics to induce acceptance of the British Crown by the Pondo people.

"He told the chief and his counselors of the might of the British gun, which 'would reduce those who resisted it into ashes by its smoke.' He thereupon called a few of his soldiers, who had accompanied him armed with guns to take aim at two of the fat oxen which were a few yards away. He also told the king and his counselors to watch carefully what the magic of the British gun would soon do to the oxen.

"The soldiers fired at the two oxen, killing them instantly amidst a roll of gunsmoke. When all this had been done and the oxen were lying stretched on the ground, he told the king and his counselors that the miracle of killing animals which he had just seen could be practiced on them in a few minutes and later on the whole nation if Sigcau did not sign the papers of annexation which were placed in front him.

"Armed with nothing but spears and sticks, Sigcau and his men were reluctantly compelled to sign those papers of annexation. To cover up this ugly, thievish, devilish tactic, Elliott ordered that the killed animals be skinned and cooked for the king and his men. So it was that the last resisting Xhosa-speaking people of South Africa were forced to surrender their land to the marauding British settlers." After a slight pause, the sage Pondo historian added, "History shall absolve."*

As his friend finished the narration, Dunga went on to tell how the neighbors of the AmaMpondo, the AmaMpondomise of the adjacent districts of Tsolo and Qumbu, also resisted the white settling of their land: "Sometime toward the end of the nineteenth century, the Mpondomise people were so disillusioned by the presence of the white people, who kept on carving the land into bits and inviting their kinsfolk to come over from across the Kei River to farm on the Mpondomise land, that they decided to do something about those whites who resided in the towns of Tsolo and Qumbu.

"One night the Mpondomise army invaded the town of Tsolo. When they entered the town, they killed all the adult white males, saving only women, children and missionaries. After doing this, they found white lime, used for house painting, in the

---

*I have sinced checked with the unpublished historical archives in the Cape Town Museum and found this story of the annexation of Pondoland to be accurate.

44

shops. They thought this was mealie-meal and started cooking it for a dish of porridge. Some of them became sick and weak but did not die.

"They ordered the saved white wives and children to start on foot towards Umtata where they would be cared for by their kin. Meanwhile, they, the Mpondomise army, were to proceed across the Tsitsa River to the town of Qumbu to repeat their actions.

"One Mpondomise man, who had worked for one of the saved missionaries in Tsolo, galloped on his master's horse to Qumbu to warn the whites about the killing and looting of the oncoming 'savages.' A brother of his also galloped another horse in a different direction, to Umtata, to warn Sir Henry and his gang of what had happened and to see if they could not help.

"The group of men heading for Qumbu were slowed down by their great physical distress from the lime they had eaten. Both horseback envoys—riding like spies to Qumbu and Umtata—got to their respective destinations before the Mpondomise army arrived. Sir Henry was able to dispatch some of his British soldiers to evacuate what was left of the whites in Tsolo and all the whites in Qumbu before the arrival of the Mpondomise army, some of whom were arrested en route to Qumbu.

"The families of the two would-be saviors of the British whites were rewarded with two farms in the Tsolo district. The families used those farms for two generations. Their descendants still live in the Transkei today and I know them well but may not mention their names for security's sake. Indeed, they have been forgiven, but the act of their treachery will never be forgotten."

The moral lesson I learned from this story is how good-hearted and good-natured the Mpondomise people are. Witness how they carefully screened the women, children and missionaries from the real culprits, the men who carried the guns and became the legal administrators of the British Crown; also witness how they saved the missionaries under the belief that these people were simply messengers of God.

By the time this historical account of the whites forcibly taking possession of the land had finished, it was almost dusk. Seriously absorbed in these stories, we were still sitting near the cattle kraal. Fortunately, a full moon appeared with enough bright light for us to continue our conversation until midnight. The women had brought us food, beer and mutton. Quite a few other village men who had been attracted to Dunga's homestead by the sight of strange horses had joined us, followed by a few women, who might have been their wives, carrying some *lalas,* or gourd's, full of beer.

Now the conversation broadened, each man relating what he knew of the Mpondomise chiefs and, in general, what happened during the Majola dynasty. Father Dunga related the legend of Mhlontlo, the Mpondomise king and son of Matiwane. He was the most illustrious of the Mpondomise warrior-kings toward the end of the nineteenth century and was renowned for his magical powers.

According to legend, when Mhlontlo was being doctored in order to make him immune to witchcraft, he was locked in a special *phemphe,* or small thatched hut, which was then burned down completely. But lo and behold, Mhlontlo emerged unscathed, without a mark on his body! The medicine man stood amazed and said, "Mhlontlo, you are the first king to go through this ordeal. I have doctored other kings, but when it came to the burning of the phempe, invariably the courage deserted them and they refused to endure the ordeal of fire. Since you have shown this valor and endurance, I say that no bullet will ever have the power to slay you."

Dunga went on: "When, during Honi's War, the white soldiers surrounded Mhlontlo in a cave and aimed their guns at him, they failed to kill him, for he was guarded by two dogs—nobody knows from whence they came—who caught the white men's bullets and swallowed them."

The conversation ended with the arrival of the host's flock of sheep. When the flock entered the fold, Dunga followed, together with some herdboys. The boys caught a huge, eight-toothed *wether,* or castrated ram, and dragged it by the horns towards Babana, the leader of our party. After the host said a few words of welcome to us, enjoining us to eat this "small meat" and resume our journey, one junior man from my party and myself proceeded to slaughter the sheep. It was customary in the Transkei in those days that strangers from a faraway land be accorded the full respect of all social entertainments once they were known and liked by the host.

We had had a wonderful history lesson, good companionship with other men, and all the food and drink we could enjoy. What more was needed to call this an evening worthy to recount, I do not know. We were very late getting to sleep, but at dawn the following day our search for a diviner continued.

Finally we reached Cele Village, on the border of Pondoland and Natal. People had told us that the woman there "solved problems," and we eventually came to the diviner's homestead. Without our introducing ourselves, this woman of Cele immediately told us that we were visiting her in regard to the illness of some man. "What you have come for is this: a man is very sick. He is coughing, dreaming much, crying in his sleep." She then analyzed and diagnosed the nature of the man's illness very closely, giving the symptoms we had seen at home. She spread a set of white and black bones on the floor and kept tossing them as if playing dice. Finally, all the bones came to a standstill except one black one, which rolled a couple of times more than the rest.

A voice from the thatched roof whistled a woman's name which was familiar to us. The diviner told us that if we could identify the name from the whistling, that was the name of the person who had bewitched the sick man back home. Whether this was clairvoyance or ventriloquism I have never been able to decide. The whistling sound of a woman's name we interpreted to be "Majali." When one of our party asked the diviner to confirm that it was Majali, she answered that the actual name would never come from her mouth. It was for us to puzzle out what the *milozi,* or whistler, had said. These experts were never in the habit of committing themselves verbally by naming the witch, probably a way of exculpating themselves in case the bewitchers brought suit against them for defamation of character. Before we left, the head of the party paid the diviner five shillings, her usual fee.

We returned home, this time in two days instead of three because we did not have to stop and ask for directions. The day after our arrival, the village folk, men and women, were assembled at the sick man's homestead to hear our report. All the members of our party had been sworn to secrecy; we were not to discuss our journey with anyone before the leader of our group had reported to the whole village at the meeting where Majali and her husband would be present.

When Majali was named the culprit responsible for the sickness of the village elder, her husband slowly stood up and asked that two men and one woman accompany him to his house, where they were to pack up all the belongings of his wife and bring them back to the group. Within an hour they returned with all of Majali's belongings. The husband handed these to Majali, publicly disclaimed her as his wife and said, "Disappear from my face and the faces of all these villagers. Go to a 'never-never land' where none of us will ever see you again." Thus Majali was ostracized from the village.

Two village boys were ordered to help her carry her belongings as far as the border of the village. Majali, in tears, was escorted by the boys, who returned the following day to say they had left her at sunset, heading east across the Nqabeni River. Nothing was ever heard from Majali, at least until I left that part of the country nine years later. Rumor had it that she migrated to the heart of Zululand, far from any people who might know anything about her past life. She could have started a new life, in a new land, among strange people of different customs and minds. She left the village of her birth in disgrace and unlamented.

Perhaps it should be mentioned that men as well as women were "smelled out" by the diviners in those days. The women were treated gently compared to the punishment meted out to the men, who were stoned, beaten and sometimes even killed while being chased away.

It seemed to me that society would be better without witch-hunting and divination; however, these may be historically and sociologically justifiable for the culture. The experiences of my youth afforded me much to reflect upon as I later compared the social dramas of different societies and cultures.

4

Lovedale Missionary Institute

After all the events of the summer holidays had been consummated, I was ready to proceed to Lovedale Missionary Institute for my high school education. The bus route to Lovedale took me to Umtata, where I was to catch a train to Alice, a small city in the Ciskei region of the Cape Province. As in earlier days, the bus went through Port St. Johns, where it once again made a stop a few miles out of town to allow us time to fill our provision baskets with as much fruit as we needed. I filled my basket to the brim until it "overfloweth" like in the good old days when I was en route to St. Johns.

I had written my old friends at St. Johns asking them to meet me at the railway station on the day I would entrain and, as sure as fate, they were there to meet me and bid me farewell, wishing me Godspeed in that new world, the country of the Ngqikas where Lovedale was situated. This area was generally known to Africans as KwaNgqika—the land of Ngqika, a famous Xhosa king. Ngqika's popularity was enhanced among the Xhosa people all over the Cape when he refused to take sides during the feud between the British and the Dutch over possession of a certain section of land in the Ciskei. When the British general approached Ngqika to ask for help in the white civil dispute over the land, which they had stealthily expropriated from Africans, Ngqika replied, "I cannot involve myself in issues and affairs that do not pertain to black people."

49

That incident was recorded in a very popular African song which topped the list of school favorites for decades. I myself had sung this song many times as a school boy. We all had very great respect for this king, who initiated the principle of non-collaboration with the settlers. I looked forward to stepping on the land of that great man of Africa.

Lovedale was one of the earliest Western educational institutions established in southern Africa, founded in the beginning of the nineteenth century by Dr. Love, a Scottish missionary. I use the term "Western" because there had been institutions of informal and formal learning long before the arrival of the first white men. Zimbabwe, for instance, was founded as early as AD 1100, and ruins there show many traces of learning. Sophisticated drawings and various kinds of script-writing on stone are still discernible today in caves in parts of Botswana and around the Western Cape. These indicate that the aborigines, the AbaThwa and Khoikhon (the so-called Bushmen and Hottentots), were able to communicate using a non-verbal medium. When I worked as a school teacher in the Zwenshambe area of northern Botswana, I would go guinea-fowl hunting on weekends and was fascinated and captivated by the drawings and script-writings I found in this area and could not decipher. These writings are artifacts, and the fact that they have not been deciphered does not render them any less useful or credible than the hieroglyphics used in Egypt before Christ was born.

The Lovedale area is known as eDikeni, from *dike*, meaning a fertile valley. It was extremely fertile around the Thyume River, which divides Lovedale from Fort Hare University. To the east of Lovedale and Fort Hare is Sandile's Kop, and to the west is Noncampa Hill on the way to Healdtown Institution, about ten miles from Lovedale. The Thyume River flows steadily from the direction of the Hogsback Mountains and finally erupts into the blue Indian Ocean. Throughout Ngqikaland, it is fed along the way by smaller tributaries from the Middledrift area (eXesi), King Williamstown (eQonce) and Peddie (eNgqushwa). As the Thyume River meanders toward the Indian Ocean, growing fat from the waters of the smaller rivers, it attracts more and more admirers of its splendor, and the local boys rush around it to enjoy swimming in the nude at some spots and fishing at others.

After the emotional and fraternal farewells at the Umtata Station, the train finally left for Alice. We had a long stop at Blaney Railway Junction, where we met a lot of other students from other provinces in South Africa: the Orange Free State, the Transvaal and Natal—and even from other countries. There were some pretty girls among them, but in no way could they surpass those Transkeian girls in our midst, who looked as if they bathed in milk and honey.

The train's final destination was Port Elizabeth, so we parted ways on the evening of the following day. At the railway station minutes from Lovedale, I was met by my Uncle Monde, who was a senior at the Teacher Training School. New students were accommodated in different dormitories according to the regions from which we came. I lived in Shaw House, which was specifically for Transkeians. Other dormitories included Steward House for students from the eastern and western Cape, and Henderson for those from Jo'burg and the then-British territories such as Botswana, Lesotho and the Rhodesias. This arrangement left much to be desired, as it tended to encourage the regionalism that already bordered on tribalism.

Another anachronistic arrangement in the boarding system at Lovedale, abolished just before our arrival, was an established class differentiation of eating tables in the dining room based on economic status. There had been three categories: a table for those who paid the highest fees of about thirty-five pounds a year, which included sons of chiefs, kings and other so-called nobility and rich men; an eating table for the middle class, sons of professionals such as teachers, nurses, etc., who paid about twenty-five pounds a year; and a lower-class table where the majority of the students sat. This final table was the cheapest, affordable by the average parents who wanted to send their youngsters to school. I am told students used to refer to this lower-class table as the "table of the masses."

Naturally, these divisions tended to create more animosity than brotherhood among the students. The living and boarding arrangements tended to encourage regionalism and ethnic divisions, while the dining room arrangements emphasized and displayed class identity according to economic and political standards. This encouragement of class distinction was foreign to the average African community, where we were taught at an early age to be "our brother's keeper." Living communally and sharing whatever amenities we had was ingrained in most of us.

Fortunately the class divisions in the dining room at Lovedale were abolished in the early forties; the ethnic division in living accomodation still existed but had not caused any conflict between students since the big 1946 Lovedale students' strike, caused by the poor quality of the food. A few students, notably from houses other than Shaw House—students from the Transkei were notoriously close-lipped and never gave any information to Western authorities—were made to testify against other students in the inquiry that was held following the aftermath of the strike. Unfortunately, the authorities had enticed some students to testify under the threat of permanent expulsion. Since their homes were so far away from the Cape Province, making it extremely expensive to return home without graduating, and since their train fares coming from home would take much longer to reach them while the school was temporarily closed, they testified against their colleagues. The school was temporarily closed and everyone sent home to reapply; these students, however, were given a reprieve and a special dispensation to remain at the institution and reapply "from within."

When the rest of the students were readmitted later that year, all the students met to discuss in a friendly atmosphere "with malice towards none and goodness for all," the political aspect of the divide-and-rule method of pitting one group against the other. As a result, by the time we got to Lovedale, there was a very healthy spirit of brother- and sisterhood among the students. The dormitory Balkanization was almost meaningless.

High school at Lovedale was similar to any American high school except that we were a far more disciplined group. This discipline was not necessarily imposed by the authorities but rather something we had grown up with and learned from our homes and junior secondary schools. Teachers were very highly respected as *bafundisi,* or givers of education. The five-day week was devoted to school work and school-related activities.

For two full years I studied English, Xhosa, history, mathematics, physics and chemistry. My certificate was issued by the Joint Matriculation Board and entitled me to apply for entrance to any university in South Africa or England, since at that time we took exactly the same exams as whites. During the week we had sports practices, chores such as cleaning the school grounds, choir practice and club activities. The latter included the Independent Order of True Templers (IOTT), organized against overindulgence in alcoholic beverages, known to students as "I Only Take Tea." Another organization was the Brotherhood of Honor, which taught older boys and girls all about sex, its virtues and its vices. We also had weekly debating societies. All extracurricular activities were headed by one or two staff members.

Relationships with girls were relegated to Saturday afternoons on the sports fields. We enjoyed watching rugby, soccer and cricket, depending on the season, but we enjoyed watching and meeting girls even more. The same was true on Sunday. More often than not, while the preacher would be threatening us about the "world to come," we would be concentrating our glances on those beautiful, cleanly dressed girls listening to the preacher. During Easter holidays, staff members planned coeducational lunches to stress and cultivate the best table manners. We boys tried very hard to master the social graces, mainly to impress those perfect young women. We were learning a great deal about life both inside and outside the classroom.

Political Indoctrination from Across the River

Just across the Thyume River and, in fact, within a stone's throw of Lovedale, was the University College of Fort Hare, founded in 1916 by missionaries attached to Lovedale. From the center of Lovedale it took about fifteen minutes to cross the Chalmer's Bridge to Fort Hare. For the members of the African National Congress Youth League, 1949 was a year of great political activity. On weekends, the leading members of the League regularly visited our dormitories to initiate us into the intricacies and complexities of African nationalism. Regular "indoctrinators" included Mangaliso Robert Sobukwe, the founder-president of the Pan-Africanist Congress of Azania and then-president of the College Students Representative Council; Duma Nokwe, who was to become secretary-general of the African National Congress; Godfrey Pitje, now an attorney, and others. These were young men who were considered firebrands of nationalism not only on the campus of Fort Hare but throughout the nation. If they did not visit our dormitories, they would have us gather around them on Saturday afternoons at the sports field or near the "Tuck Shop," where we did our afternoon shopping for candy and other small items.

We thoroughly enjoyed these serious study groups. We used to look forward to weekends, when we would learn about the national situation as well as our past heroes: Tshaka, Moshoeshe, Sekukuni, Makana and many others whose greatness was neither mentioned nor emphasized in our European-oriented history books. Our elder brothers would always warn us to read the Bible very objectively because "the white man brought us the Bible at the same time he was carrying a gun with him. We had the land, the wealth, and all the livestock. Now the white man has all the land, most of the livestock and all the wealth. All that we were left is the Bible. Do not sheepishly swallow everything in it. Most of it is excellent reading. For example, 'Do unto others as you would have others do unto you'." They emphasized the fact that we worked for the white man and did many good things for him, but did he reciprocate? We were left to puzzle out such questions until the following meeting.

We had many meetings on different political, religious and other, more down-to-earth topics; there was never a dull moment when we were with those leaders. We came to realize that history books about Africa and Africans were tainted, for their perspective was almost exclusively European. Of course, Europeans presented their side of the story to suit their purposes, which included their rationalizations for grabbing African land using vicious exploitative tactics. When they arrived for the first time in Cape Town in 1652, they did not carry any land or cattle in their ships, yet now they were claiming all the land as theirs and were accusing the Africans of stealing cattle. Who stole whose land and cattle? Furthermore, when Europeans wrote about our past kings and heroes, they called Tshaka a "savage"; we regard Tshaka as a military genius. "What manner of studying history is this?" our study group leaders would ask. This excellent, fresh food for thought both supplemented our growing body of knowledge and disgorged some of the inexplicable fallacies of history as represented by the white man. Many African patriots still consider the rewriting of our history to be of great priority, and this generation is in the process of doing just that. There is so much to do to correct and clarify the records of history; the time must be now, before those who know and recognize the truth join their ancestors.

In education I found a concrete form of expression for my political beliefs. Throughout our youth, my friends and I had looked upon education as a vehicle for contributing to our country by improving the systems in control of it. The stories told to us by the men in the village informed us of the wrongs enacted against us by the white man and gave us a growing perspective of the problems we would encounter in our adulthood. Formal education would give us the means to combat these wrongs and so better the lives of our families, friends and countrymen.

The conspiracy to "murder" education had been going on for decades in southern Africa. As early as 1935 the Committee on Native Education, appointed by the South African government to study the question of education for the African population, had concluded that not much could be done to improve the quality of African education. Indeed, what little education the Africans had received so far was good enough since it was in keeping with the prevailing attitude that only white children deserved formal education. The Committee declared: "The education of the white child prepares him for life in a dominant society and the education of the black child for a subordinate society.... The limits of native education form part of the social and economic structure of the society."[1]

In 1948, following the electoral victory (in the all-white general elections) of the Nationalist Party, the Christian National Education Manifesto was published. According to the CNEM, "God ... willed separate nations and peoples, and He gave to each separate nation and people its special vocation, task and gifts.''[2] These policies were further promoted when the government appointed a commission on native education called the Eiselen Commission, headed by Dr. W.W.M. Eiselen, a faithful member of the Afrikaner Nationalist Party.

Early in October of 1949 I was listening to a history lecture when the teacher was interrupted by a visit from the nine-member Eiselen Commission. A few of us were called upon to testify, involuntarily, before that body of doom for African education. The chairman of the Commission asked us questions such as:

Does it not make you feel uncomfortable to sit in a class with a child not of your tribe?

Don't you think the white man's mathematics is rather a waste of time and you'd rather just learn arithmetic to count your money, goats, pigs, fowls and cattle, and thereafter be done with the white man's counting system?

Do you not enjoy your own home-cooked food from clay pots from the fire of dry cow-dung and forest wood rather than that dry bread from the shop which is smoked in a white man's wood stove?

Do you not think your own witch doctors do a better job healing you when you are sick rather than the white doctor who causes you more pains by pricking you with those painful needles? (The questioner would then express the uselessness of studying chemistry, physics, physiology and other related courses which would prepare one for a career in medicine.)

Do you not think there is more fresh air out in the countryside rather than in the white man's crowded cities? Wouldn't you rather stay there in order to live longer? (This would prepare the young mind to accept being segregated in the bantustans, which are the most infertile, barren part of South Africa.)

These commissioners of the Dark Ages remained at Lovedale asking students hundreds of such myopic questions. Our answers were almost universally no's, but, like all ambassadors of falsehood and intellectual dishonesty, they wrote down what they wanted to hear. No one was ever allowed to have his or her answers read back. After I had been grilled for about forty-five minutes, I requested my answers and comments be read back to me. The single black "Uncle Tom" member of the commission replied for the white bosses: "The report of your answers will be sent back to you from Pretoria after the authorities have approved your replies." This was in 1949. I am still waiting for that transcript today.

The whole purpose of Bantu Education was to remove African children from even the possibility of acquiring a normal education, instead turning them into mechanical robots, "drawers of water and hewers of wood." Most simply expressed, the South African government took control of African education to forever perpetuate the despicable policies of apartheid.

After the Bantu Education Act was passed in 1953, just before I left college, I had occasion to read it together with the original Eiselen Commission Report. Some theorize that a child's mind is a *tabula rasa,* a clean slate on which anything can be written. African children were to have imprinted on their minds the idea that they were inferior to whites and thus must do their bidding. The authors of Bantu Education hoped to make an African child a docile robot willing to do anything at the command of the white man. What a rude awakening these "masters" were to receive several years later when, among other things, students engaged in uprisings in Soweto in 1976, clearly spelling out the impossibility of the imposition of these ideas via a "separate and unequal" education.

Prior to the passage of the Bantu Education Act, the control of African education was divided among the provincial administrations, the missionary societies and the people themselves. Its funding was largely by voluntary contributions from Christian missions and the African parents. Black South Africans were eager for the kind of education that they saw freely lavished upon the white population, and most schools for Africans had been built willingly as self-help projects by the villagers themselves. Education was and still is neither free nor compulsory for Africans, yet there had always been the hope that someday blacks and whites would together receive the same education in order to have the opportunity to reach the same or equal positions in the community and the society.

The Bantu Education Act completely ended that dream.* The government took over the sole control and direction of African education. Dr. D.G.S. Mtimkulu, a reputable African educator, warned the government that Africans were unlikely to accept Bantu Education because they sought for integration into the democratic structure and institutions of the country. To Africans, he said, one of the most effective ways of achieving that integration was through education—education which was "essentially no different from, or inferior to, that of other sections of the community."[3]

On the other hand, Dr. H.F. Verwoerd, later Prime Minister, then Minister of Native Affairs, held that prior to Bantu Education the African had been miseducated and misled by being shown "the green pastures of European society in which he is not allowed to graze."[4] Dr. Verwoerd stressed that education must train and teach people "in accordance with their opportunities in life, according to the sphere in which they live." In keeping with the government's plan for South Africa, he continued, there was "no place for the Bantu in the European community above the level of certain forms of labor." Consequently, the regime had decided that education for Africans should "stand with both feet in the Reserves [later to become the bantustans] and have its roots in the spirit and being of a Bantu society."[5]

---

*After having "worked over" primary and secondary education, the planners of Bantu Education moved to the universities with the passage in 1959 of the Extension of University Education Act. Just the opposite of extending education, this act closed the entrance of blacks to Rhodes University, the University of Natal and other English universities that had previously accepted black students. The aims of apartheid were furthered by the establishment of five non-white universities: the University of the Western Cape for coloreds; the University of Durban-Westville for Indians; the University of the North at Turfloop for Sothos, Tswanas, Ndebeles, Vendas, Shagaans and Tsongas; the University of Zululand and Ngoye for Zulus and Swazis; and the University of Fort Hare for Xhosas. Blacks could also study through correspondence courses with the University of South Africa.

The education that I and my classmates received at Fort Hare is no more. University standards have deteriorated under Bantu Education, and for many, little learning takes place in the classroom.

Dr. Verwoerd further contended that there existed sound reasons for a special kind of education for an African child. The common knowledge of a white child, he asserted, was different from that of an African child. For that reason Bantu Education ought to be different "because it has as its starting point other sources and other kinds of knowledge." He emphasized that Bantu Education should not clash with government policies, and warned that ". . . if the native in South Africa today in any kind of school in existence is being taught to expect that he will live his adult life under a policy of equal rights, he is making a big mistake."[6]

Another subsequent minister of Bantu Education, W.A. Maree, told Parliament that Africans must be so educated that they would not want to become imitators of the whites but "they will want to remain Bantu."[7]

As the Bantu Education Act came into effect in 1954, it was apparent that indeed the central government planned to control all facets of African education as was provided in the law. Every one of the great variety of schools for "natives" had to be registered with the minister of Bantu Education. The minister was also empowered to make regulations regarding the control of schools, the conditions of service of teachers, the media of instruction, the appropriation of school funds and many other matters.

In spite of protests and demonstrations throughout the country by liberation organizations, student and teacher unions and all kinds of committees against Bantu Education, the government sped ahead with its program. The educational syllabus and curriculum were so readjusted that emphasis was placed wholly on ethnicity in order to accelerate and encourage the tribal affinity of the different groups. Certain courses had to be included and emphasized in the curriculum: the Bible to teach obedience and docility, fear of God and fear of the white man; agriculture or some form of soil cultivation to make worthy cultivators of the rich soil of South Africa in order to produce crops for the settlers; and handwork of any kind, as well as carpentry and cooking. After all, 99 percent of South African whites do not cook but employ blacks to cook for them and for their animal pets. An ethnic language and one official language—either English or Afrikaans—were required. No black objected to learning vernacular languages and developing them scientifically, as other languages had been enlarged, while being exposed to other tongues and additional terminology. But the oppressors' language was hated; it seemed clear that Afrikaans was to be used so that the African population would be able to follow commands when in contact with whites. Physics, chemistry, mathematics and the social sciences were all de-emphasized as they really "did not prepare the native child for the world in which he lives." J.N. LeRoux, a Broederbond* leader, had urged Parliament not to give Africans any academic education because, he wondered, "Who is going to do the manual labor in this country?"[8]

This was all still in the future. When I graduated from Fort Hare University in November 1953, ready to enter the teaching profession, it was into this world of education polluted by conservative theories that I became embroiled. But in 1949, it was not too difficult to see the groundwork being layed for these loathsome injustices.

A week before I took my final examinations at the end of October, my beloved father died. I could not even attend the funeral because I would have had to spend about five days traveling to and from Eastern Pondoland, where he had died suddenly after being discharged from Holy Cross Hospital. All I could say was simply, "Such a sleep he sleeps, the man I loved."

I managed to pass my exams in the First Class (so-called by the British). When we had completed our finals we, as senior boys, were allowed to attend a farewell social function for the graduating class at Fort Hare: the "Completors Social." The main speaker was Mangaliso Robert Sobukwe, whom we knew and idolized as our leader from the visits he had paid to Lovedale during the course of the year. I was sitting on one of

---

*Broederbond, literally meaning "league of brothers," is an exclusive, all-white, male organization established in 1918 to promote Afrikaner people and their interests. It is regarded by almost all blacks and some whites as an extreme right-wing, racist group similar to the Ku Klux Klan in the United States.

the chairs at the back of the dining hall when he spoke, and I still remember his speech on that memorable night as if it were delivered yesterday; it left an impression on me as no other had in my youth. It was a timeless address, as applicable today as it was then to universities in South Africa and even to universities anywhere in the world that aim to inspire black students to change the conditions of racism and oppression still plaguing the world. Such a courageous, clear-cut challenge to the roots of apartheid must be quoted here for all to read.

Sobukwe first reviewed the "doings within the college" from the previous year. He commented critically on the path and policies of the college, which he felt required immediate attention and change: "It has always been my feeling that if the intention of the trustees of the College is to make it an African college or university, as I have been informed it is, then the Department of African Studies must be more highly and rapidly developed. Fort Hare must become the center of African Studies to which students in African Studies should come from all over Africa. We should also have a Department of Economics and Sociology. A nation, to be a nation, needs specialists in these things. . . .

"I would like to know exactly what the College understands by "trusteeship." I understand by trusteeship the preparation of the African ward for eventual management and leadership of the College. But nothing in the policy of the College points in this direction. After the College has been in existence for thirty years, the ratio of Europeans to Africans is four to one. And we are told that in ten years' time we might become an independent university. Are we to understand that an African university is predominantly guided by European thought and strongly influenced by European staff?

"I said last year that Fort Hare must be to the African what Stellenbosch is to the Afrikaner. It must be the barometer of African thought. It is interesting to note that the theory of apartheid, which is today the dominating ideology of the State, was worked out at Stellenbosch by Eiselen and his colleagues. That same Eiselen is Secretary for Native Affairs. But the important thing is that Stellenbosch is not only the expression of Afrikaner thought and feeling but is also the embodiment of their aspiration. So also must Fort Hare express and lead African thought. The College has remained mute on matters deeply affecting the Africans, because, we learn, it feared to annoy the nationalist government.

"I said last year that our whole life in South Africa is politics, and that contention was severely criticized. But the truth of that statement has been proved in the course of this year.... We have heard responsible preachers deplore the deterioration of race-relations in this country and suggest cooperation as a solution.... A number of speakers in our Wednesday assembly have condemned this 'naughty spirit of nationalism and non-cooperation' and have told us of the wonderful things that have been done for us, forgetting, of course, that what they say has been done for the Africans, the Africans have achieved for themselves in spite of the South African government. The point I am trying to make is, that was politics, whether we loved it or not, so that we can no longer pretend that there is a proper place and a proper occasion for politics. During the war it was clearly demonstrated that in South Africa, at least, politics does not stop this side of the grave. A number of African soldiers were buried in the same trench as European soldiers. A few days afterwards, word came from the high command that the bodies of the Africans should be removed and buried in another trench. Apartheid must be maintained even on the road to eternity."

Sobukwe directly addressed every listener when he charged us to use our education to build a nation for the people: "A word to those who are remaining behind. You have seen by now what education means to us: the identification of ourselves with the masses. Education to us means service to Africa. In whatever branch of learning you are, you are there for Africa. You have a mission; we all have a mission. A nation to build we have, a God to glorify, a contribution clear to make towards the blessing of mankind. We must be the embodiment of our people's aspirations. And all we are required to do is to show the light and the masses will find the way....

"We will watch you, too. We have been reminded time and again of fellows who, while at College, were radicals, and as soon as they got outside became the spineless stooges and screeching megaphones of white Herrenvolkism or else became disgruntled and disillusioned objects of pity. My contention is: those fellows never were radicals. They were anti-white. And as Marcus Garvey says, 'You cannot grow beyond your thoughts. If your thoughts are those of a slave, you will remain a slave. If your thoughts go skin-deep, your mental development will remain skin-deep.'

"Moreover, a doctrine of hate can never take people anywhere. It is too exacting. It warps the mind. That is why we preach the doctrine of love, love for Africa. We can never do enough for Africa, nor can we love her enough. The more we do for her, the more we wish to do. And I am sure that I am speaking for the whole of young Africa when I say that we are prepared to work with any man who is fighting for the liberation of Africa *within our lifetime*...."

Using an historical and philosophical approach, Sobukwe briefly explained the broad principles of the decay of nations and his belief in the inevitability of African development and strength: "This is a difficult period to analyze.... We are witnessing today the disintegration of old empires and the integration of new communities. We are seeing today the germination of the seeds of decay inherent in capitalism; we discern the first shoots of the tree of socialism....

"We are seeing within our own day the second rape of Africa, a determined effort by imperialist powers to dig their claws still deeper into the flesh of the squirming victim. But this time the imperialism we see is not the naked, brutal, mercantile imperialism of the seventeenth and eighteenth centuries. It is a more subtle one—financial and economic imperialism under the guise of a tempting slogan, 'the development of backward areas and peoples.' The old order is changing, ushering in a new order. The great revolution has started, and Africa is the field of operation. Allow me at this juncture to quote a few lines from the Methodist hymn-book:

> *Once to every man and nation*
> *Comes the moment to decide,*
> *In the strife of truth with falsehood*
> *For the good or evil side....*

Then to side with truth is noble
When we share her wretched crust,
Ere her cause bring fame and profit
And 'tis prosperous to be just.
Then it is the brave man chooses
While the coward stands aside,
'Til the multitude make virtue
Of the faith they had denied.

The cowards are still standing aside and the brave have made their choice. We have made our choice. And we have chosen African nationalism because of its deep human significance, because of its inevitability and necessity to world progress. World civilization will not be complete until the African has made his full contribution. And even as the dying so-called Roman civilization received new life from the barbarians, so also will the decaying so-called western civilization find a new and purer life from Africa.

"I wish to make it clear again that we are anti-nobody. We are pro-Africa. We breath, we dream, we live Africa, because Africa and humanity are inseparable. It is only by doing the same that the minorities in this land, the European, colored and Indian, can secure mental and spiritual freedom. On the liberation of the African depends the liberation of the whole world. The future of the world lies with the oppressed, and the Africans are the most oppressed people on earth, not only in the continent of Africa but also in America and the West Indies. We have been accused of blood-thirstiness because we preach 'non-collaboration.' I wish to state here tonight that that is the only course open to us. History has taught us that a group in power has never voluntarily relinquished its position. It has always been forced to do so. And we do not expect miracles to happen in Africa. It is necessary for human progress that Africa be fully developed, and only the African can do so. . . .

"Let me plead with you, lovers of my Africa, to carry with you into the world the vision of a new Africa, an Africa reborn, an Africa rejuvenated, and Africa re-created, young *Africa*."

Sobukwe concluded his speech with words which were to become oft-quoted at Pan-Africanist meetings: "These things shall be, says the psalmist: Africa will be free. The wheel of progress revolves relentlessly. And all the nations of the world take their turn at the field-glass of human destiny. Africa will not retreat! Africa will not compromise! Africa will not relent! Africa will not equivocate! And She will be heard! *Remember Africa!*"*

I felt like a born-again Christian. The clarion call of "Remember Africa" had been issued, never to be forgotten. What black could turn away from that challenge/hope/dream/vision of Sobukwe's? There and then, I joined Sobukwe in the physical and intellectual pursuit of freedom for my people. Even today in the United States, I still remember Africa and come what may, I am destined to return to South Africa, to make it a free Azania.

The following year I was to cross the Thyume River to Fort Hare, not as a visitor this time but as an enrolled student. I looked forward to college education and the opportunity to expand upon the words of wisdom I had heard from Sobukwe on the very spot where they had been delivered. Many ideas and principles had become part of me during my two years at Lovedale; I would carry them with me to Fort Hare University and beyond.

Speeches of Mangaliso Sobukwe from 1949-1959 and Other Documents of the Pan-Africanist Congress of Azania, PAC Observer Mission to the United Nations, New York.

5

Fort Hare University, Training Ground for Independence

Soon after my arrival at Fort Hare in 1950, I learned that the university buildings were originally constructed by the British for use as a fort in the nineteenth century. For several decades, these buildings served to protect a handful of white traders and missionaries against the "marauding Xhosas" in a land that was once Xhosa and has rapidly become occupied by white settlers. Remnants of the fort—stone foundations, broken brick walls, fireplaces—were still preserved, fenced in by barbed wire between the Anglican hostel of Beda Hall and the Presbyterian hostel of Iona, unfortunate reminders of the bitter past.

Fort Hare was opened as a learning center for Africans and children of white missionaries in 1916. Before and during the time I spent there, the college attracted students from all over southern and central Africa; for many years it was the only center for higher learning in the whole southern and central African area. Many past and present leaders of Africa have passed through its gates. To give but a few examples, the short-tenured president of Uganda, Yusuf Lule, once held the one-mile record at Fort Hare. The late president of Botswana, Seretse Khama, attended both Lovedale and Fort Hare. The internationally known Z.K. Matthews was the only black holding a full professorship at Fort Hare during my days there. He had been the first black student to graduate from Fort Hare in 1923.*

Other black political leaders from South Africa who studied at Fort Hare are: Oliver Tambo, acting president of the African National Congress; Govan Mbeki, an ANC political figure given life imprisonment for his political activities; and Dennis Brutus, known for his anti-apartheid sports activities. Well-known figures of later years whom I knew while I attended Fort Hare included the former minister of justice in Malawi, Orton Chirwa; while a Fort Harian he was called "Philosopher" since he always philosophized in his debates and conversations. We all got to know each other quite well, especially those of us of the same religious faith. Anglicans (my religious affiliation) and Catholics had mass together. Many of us noted that Robert Mugabe, later to become prime minister of Zimbabwe, took Holy Communion every Sunday and sometimes during the week, so he earned the nickname "Too Christian."

Indeed, most black college graduates of the thirties, forties and early fifties in southern Africa either received their university education at Fort Hare or some English or American university, since South African white universities never opened their doors to blacks for higher learning.

Luckily, boarding and lodging arrangements at Fort Hare were not assigned along ethnic lines, as had been the case at Lovedale, which might have prevented the free exchange of ideas among those of us from different countries. Instead, our division was based on denominational grounds. Roman Catholics and Anglicans were accomodated at Beda Hall, Methodists at Wesley Hall, and Baptists, Presbyterians and the

---

*Later, in 1960, Z.K. Matthews left his professorship because of his disgust with the Extension of University Education Act. He opened up a law office in Alice and became secretary of the World Council of Churches. When Botswana became independent in 1966, it had only two secondary schools and no university; hence, there were very few educated citizens to fill the places of the departing British. Seretse Khama invited Matthews to become an ambassador to the United States and to the United Nations, and he died in Washington DC in April 1968.

rest at Iona House. This was quite a fair arrangement as far as we were concerned, since nobody took any of these boundaries too seriously. There were no religious fanatics among the university students; living accomodations were taken for what they were meant to be—places to sleep and take meals. Communication of ideas could not be contained within boundaries such as these.

The early fifties marked a period when the political winds of change were blowing violently throughout the continent. The fact that all the colonial powers had not seen fit to build colleges for their colonies turned out to be a blessing in disguise. Because of this, politically conscious youth had one spot in which to gather—Fort Hare. The giant of Africa was waking up after one hundred years or more of colonial rule by the British, French, Portuguese, Belgians and Dutch, and Fort Hare became the catalytic meeting point for the founding and expansion of a small Organization of African Unity for the southern half of the continent. All the students from these countries knew first hand what it was to be colonized. Hardly an evening passed during which groups did not meet to discuss some aspect of colonialism. The consensus of opinion among us was that the time had come when we would cease to consider ourselves "leaders of tomorrow," as had always been emphasized in high school by our missionary indoctrinators. The time was now to "take up arms against the sea of oppression." Nobody was inclined to sit on the sidelines and watch humanity itself being eroded by western vandals in the name of "western Christian civilization."

Fort Hare had become the hotbed of southern African political thought for the young militants who had gathered there for an education—and education *for what purpose* became the question. Surely not education to do the colonial masters' bidding. Of what use is education to people shackled in chains of colonialism and imperialism? We did not kid ourselves. We were still slaves and vassals of the white man who continued to hold on to our lands of birth.* Almost all of us realized that the strug-

---

*The rising tide of independence in the fifties brought forth political independence for most African nations in the sixties.

gle in South Africa was part of the greater struggle throughout the continent for the restoration of the control of their land to the African people. Any kind of education that excluded preparation for the political and/or militant takeover of our land would be useless.

In 1953 the mood was growing that Mangaliso Sobukwe was to express in 1959: *"Koda kube nini Nkosi zonk'izizwe zisinyasha phantsi kweenyawo?* [Until when, oh Lord, will all nations trample us under foot?] Until we can answer, 'No more.' We will go on, Sons and Daughters of Africa, until in every shanty, in every bunk in the compounds, in every hut in the deserted villages, in every valley and on every hilltop, the cry of African freedom and independence is heard. We will continue until we walk the streets of our land as free men and free women, our heads held high. We will go on until the day dawns when every person who is in Africa will be an African, and a man's color will be as irrelevant as is the shape of his ears. We will go on, steadfastly, relentlessly, and determinedly until the cry of 'Africa for the Africans, the Africans for humanity and humanity for God' becomes a reality; until government of the Africans by the Africans for the Africans is a *fait accompli*.... We shall become ... appreciative of the fact that:

> *There is only one man in the world,*
> *And his name is All Men.*
> *There is only one woman in all the world,*
> *And her name is All Women!*

"... Sons and Daughters of Africa, we are standing on the threshold of an historic era. We are blazing a new trail and we invite you to be, with us, creators of history. Join us in the march to freedom. March with us to independence, to independence now. Tomorrow the United States of Africa!"[10]

We used to gather very often during those years at Fort Hare, analyzing and scanning the different directions towards which we were going to embark to throw off the chains of serfdom. We drew inspiration from those who had fought the white man, those who had fallen but not in vain. We talked about heroes from the battlegrounds of Thaba Bosigu, Isandlwana,

Keiskama Hoek and Sandile's Kop, which was only a mile from Fort Hare. Discussions about our own leaders and our own history were as helpful to us as our university courses. From these we developed an appreciation of our African background.

Much of this I had already acquired, or was in the process of acquiring, from my uncle, A.C. Jordan, the same uncle who had sent me to Fort Hare, even paying my college fees. My uncle had himself graduated from Fort Hare after completing high school at Lovedale. He had taught there in 1945 before joining the faculty of the University of Cape Town the following year. A professor at the University of Wisconsin in Madison at the time of his death, he was a fine writer and academician, as was his wife, my aunt Phyllis Ntantala. Throughout my manhood, they served as an inspiration to me to strive to the best of my ability and to further other people's understanding of the history, languages and present-day conditions in southern Africa.

The total school enrollment at Fort Hare fluctuated between 250 and 300 students. About one-fifth of the staff were black; the rest were white. There were four women, including one black assistant librarian. During my first three years at Fort Hare, I concentrated on my studies, majoring in history and philosophy. My minors were English, Xhosa, native law and administration, Latin and political science.

I liked my history and Latin teacher, Professor Jacobs, very much. His examination questions seemed more like riddles and puzzles than the straight-forward regurgitation of facts to which we were accustomed. For example, one time he asked about the effect of the French Revolution on some European countries during the eighteenth century, but he phrased his question thus: "When France sneezed, the whole of Europe caught fever—discuss." On another exam he asked about the cosmopolitan nature of the Roman Empire: "The Holy Roman Empire was neither holy, nor Roman, nor an empire—discuss." Some of us really enjoyed these creative questions which allowed for discussion supported by personal observations and not just the reproduction of what was in the book.

I found that both my majors, history and philosophy, allowed free, independent and original observation, and these courses I appreciated most of all. Unfortunately, we did not have as much contact with our white teachers as they and we would have liked because of the apartheid laws which limited social contact.

At the end of each school year, which was both our longest break from university studies and our Christmas holiday, I went to my aunt and uncle's home in Cape Town. This extended period from the end of November to the end of February gave me the opportunity to get a job and to visit Cape Town, a city I enjoyed very much. This also was an occasion to extend my studies within the different youth organizations, such as the New Era Fellowship, which trained youths in the basic tenets of Marxism. Although we had such a serious purpose, like most young people in organizations throughout the world we would have parties and other such social gatherings on weekends. A combination of factors determined that these were mixed social gatherings: Marxist organizations were always non-racial, and Cape Town itself was one of the most "liberal" of South African cities. The police usually did not harass those attending as they did elsewhere in South Africa, possibly because, of all the big cities of South Africa, Cape Town had the least number of Africans. The Western Cape was known as the home of the South African coloreds, who were very light in complexion. Besides, the University of Cape Town, the oldest and the largest university in the country, was also the most liberal in its racial outlook.

I remember an incident at one social gathering which brought into focus the predominant political and social attitudes of southern Africa during the fifties. I attended this party as one of the very few blacks in Athlone; it was also attended by many white progressive students from the University of Cape Town. The blacks at the party danced and otherwise mixed freely with the white students.

Outside the house where the party was held, a group of whites paraded, shouting, "We want Seretse Khama out of there." This was in reference to the late Sir Seretse Khama, president of Botswana, who had married a white woman, Ruth Williams, in England. Because of his marriage, he was denied the chieftainship of the Bamangwato to which he was heir. Both the English government and the Ngwato *kgotla*, or assembly, decreed that his offspring would never accede to the throne of chieftainship since his children would not be "pure Batswana."* The choral group did not insist on our departure from the party when they saw the rest of the non-Africans simply laughing and treating their name-calling as a joke. After all, they were not highly motivated to do violence; all they wanted was to be allowed in for the refreshments.

Returning for my second year at Fort Hare in February 1951, I was offered a ride by my philosophy professor, Dr. F.H. Brabant, who had also spent his holidays in Cape Town. He had to make stops in Johannesburg and Pretoria. I was only too happy to help with the driving and to have an opportunity to travel by road from Cape Town to Johannesburg, as I had never done this before. I looked forward to seeing the flat lands of the Orange Free State Province. The beautiful pasture lands and green farms stretched for miles as far as the eye could see in the Free State, as it was popularly known.

What I remembered most, however, had to do with the social life of the Boer province, not the geography. The Free State was then and still is the stronghold of Afrikaaner nationalism. All the members of Parliament, the provincial councils and even the city councils in the entire province belong to one political party, the ruling Nationalist Party.

When we stopped for lunch in the small town of Winburg, outside Bloemfontein, I was told I could not eat inside with my professor friend; I could only buy a sandwich from the kitchen at the back and eat it outside. I bought my lunch from the kitchen as directed, but when I went to sit in the car to eat it, I was told to move the car away from the sight of the dining room where all the whites were eating, including my professor. The very sight of me, a *kaffir* (the equivalent of "nigger"), would upset their appetites. Anger soon overcame my feelings of humilia-

---

*Botswana is the country of the Batswana or Betswana people. One member is called a Motswana and the language is Setswana.

When Seretse returned home with his English wife and ran for the elective office of president of an independent Botswana in 1966, he won by a landslide. He was president for fifteen years until he died in 1980.

tion at having this happen while I was traveling with my professor. When I refused to move, the white guard called the police; when I saw them, I hurriedly moved to the back. They would have arrested me for having meals in a white area. Undoubtedly, I could have been jailed in the Free State either for trespassing or at the invocation of one of their hundred or more local statutes that empower private white citizens to arrest a black on the spot for the mere suspicion that a crime is being contemplated.

When the white guard who had instructed me to move informed Dr. Brabant, he left his meal and joined me. We drove out of the city to a place away from the restaurant in order to eat. I suppose that walking out on his meal was the best the professor could do to protest apartheid.

Student Protests and Student Organizations

As the nationalist government stepped up its pace to make apartheid felt in every political, economic and social sphere, its efforts were met by student protest and reaction in both informal groups and in student organizations. One such reaction occurred when South African Governor General G.B. VanZyl, an Afrikaner and staunch proponent of apartheid, visited Fort Hare in 1951. Of course, all of the white faculty members attended his speech at the Christian Union Hall, but of the three hundred students on campus, only seven attended and one black faculty member. Those black students who attended were severly punished by some of us for recognizing the leader of the oppressors. A lynching squad under the leadership of the late Rossetta Ndziba, Temba Hleli and Gatsha Buthelezi,* presently the chief minister of KwaZulu, was formed to carry out the punishment. The seven were severly beaten with sticks, cold water was poured on their beds, and they were generally ostracized. The three leaders of the lynching squad were expelled from Fort Hare and were never allowed to re-enter.

---

*I was in Buthelezi's group and remember well his days as a militant. When I met him at a press conference in New York City in September 1982, I asked him what had become of his militancy now that his inkatha in the bantustan of

University students formed unions and organizations in the hope of achieving more clearly thought-out and defined goals. In the early fifties, the best-known group involved in championing students' rights and improvements in educational matters was the National Union of South African Students, solely representative of university students. Fort Hare was the only predominantly black university in the country; the other universities belonging to NUSAS were all-white, and all officials of NUSAS were white students. According to South African standards, this organization was quite liberal in that it included blacks and raised black issues in its forums. Most members were from English universities like the Universities of Cape Town, Witwatersrand, Rhodes and Natal. Students from the Afrikaans' universities—Stellenbosch, Pretoria, Bloemfontein—had their own student union with individual chapters that never included blacks.

The fundamental emphasis of NUSAS was the improvement of educational conditions for black and white students alike, focusing on what were essentially academic and administrative affairs. As an organization, NUSAS never sought deeply enough the root of the unbearable educational conditions for blacks, the political system that relegated Africans to the status of subhumans; in short, they did not want to bring "politics" into NUSAS.

Because NUSAS was mainly concerned with surface issues, I made a motion before the student body of 320 at the Christian Union Hall one night: "We cannot and dare not be unmindful of the very politics that militate against our people outside this hall and avoid attacking the very system of apartheid which regulates our daily lives. A body like NUSAS that does not want

---

KwaZulu works with the racist South African government. He replied, "You know, Mr. Jordan, that I support the revolution you all are trying to foment from outside. You know we cannot do it inside. Even recently, I met Tambo of the ANC in London and expressed my support. This was at his invitation. I even sent some of my religious ministers into Botswana, Mozambique and Swaziland to minister to the refugees." Without further comment, I leave the Buthelezi's with their London/Pretoria/Washington watered-down philosophies. History will absolve!

to involve itself in politics has no place for and among Africans, for it is the politics of oppression and genocide that permeates our very daily lives. If this house does not dissociate itself from a union that soft-pedals the struggle for complete liberation of our people and our people's childen, history will look amuck at us. Our children and their children will spit on our very graves for having kept company with this union which, by its very neutrality, is acquiescing to and aiding and abetting oppression. Remember, it is an unforgivable sin for good men when they see wrong to do nothing about it. I, therefore, move, Mr. Chairman, that this house secede from NUSAS forthwith and form the South African Students' Union, which will invite all students of all colors to include in their fight the eradication of Herren-volkism, oppression and all attendant factors that seek to op-press us.''

Although my motion lost by a mere ten votes, the majority of Fort Hare students individually withdrew their annual dues from NUSAS, dues which had been paid directly from tuition fees. In all fairness to NUSAS, it did "kick up some dust" by condemning Bantu Education, but that is as far as they went—NUSAS did not join the political and civic organizations roaming the countryside and agitating against the monstrosity of Bantu Education. It merely passed resolution upon resolution, generally condemning it and apartheid. Black students long since have broken away from NUSAS and formed the militant South African Students' Organization, an organization encompassing both university and high school students.

In spite of student organizations like NUSAS and the ANC Youth League, which identified with the aims of those outside the university, the believers in apartheid and Bantu Education continued practices within African educational institutions such as arrests of students, spying, security branch harassment, removal of passports and general denial of all freedoms to blacks. Many of these were in evidence at Fort Hare even in the early fifties.

One glaring example of the government prying into student affairs came in 1951 when an American lecturer, Pat Murphy, was deported by the South African government because he would often invite some of us to his house for ordinary discussions and perhaps a drink. He was one of the few university teachers who freely mixed with students at Fort Hare. At dances his attractive young wife would dance with African students, something taboo in South Africa. He was dismissed before I graduated.

We suspected that there were police spies among the students to monitor the actions of both teachers and students. Police spying on all campuses in South Africa, not only at Fort Hare, has since become common knowledge. In 1957 a student at the University of Rhodes, to which Fort Hare was affiliated, admitted he had been paid to pass information about the faculty and students to the security police. In 1959 a student at the Witwatersrand University admitted giving information on the activities of the student council to the Security Branch. During student trials and court cases in the sixties, more cases of spying were reported. At Fort Hare in 1964, instead of using an informer, the local chief of the special branch even attended, uninvited, a tea party given by a professor for his students and berrated them that it was incidents like these that created a feeling of equality. When the professor said that this was indeed his aim, the sergeant declared that the students were in a prohibited group area and then checked their passbooks. This was one way to break up a tea party and pass along the word not to hold friendly gatherings where political talk might occur.

In retrospect, it became clear that most student protests for change were sporadic, not very consequential, and lacking in continuity and durability. Students were often without leadership when their leaders graduated and left the movement or were expelled, silenced and/or imprisoned as quickly as they showed promise of persistent effort and ability to speak, organize and mobilize forces for change. On the other side, the authoritarian government was prepared to and did use any means to prevent and check all opposition, which increased with each small step forward by those students who publicly and courageously challenged the evils of the apartheid system.

A Teaching Position

In 1952, the end of my third year at Fort Hare, I received my Bachelor of Arts degree in history and philosophy. During my fourth year I completed the work required for a University Education Diploma (UED). The courses included for an education degree were: Principles of Education, Philosophy of Education, Psychology in Education, Teaching Methods (specializing in English, history and Xhosa) and Practical Teaching (called Practice Teaching in the United States). I did my practice teaching at Jabavu Secondary School, a demonstration school right at Fort Hare. After my year in education, I felt confident of my ability to enter the teaching profession and successfully hold forth in the classroom.*

During the final term of my training for the UED, I sent out applications for employment as a teacher, to commence the following year. Vacant positions in all schools, black and white, were advertised in the *Cape Education Gazette,* a journal of educational matters in the province published monthly by the Cape Education Department headquarters in Cape Town. This journal was easily accessible to all teachers and would-be teachers, whether black or white. Because of the apartheid laws, however, I could only apply to black schools, although white teachers could teach in any of the schools, white, colored, Indian or African. Non-white teachers had to apply to their respective ethnically designated schools.

Teacher training colleges, high schools and most secondary schools were managed by designated denominational churches. Applicants were selected by priests or missionaries who were *ipso facto* school managers in particular regions. My first preference was to teach at Emfundisweni Secondary School, which was closest to my home in Pondoland and was also where my parents met while training as teachers. The two other sections of the Emfundisweni Missionary Institution were for teacher vocational training. I applied for a secondary school teaching position, and I received Reverend Perry's reply to my application early in December, just before school ended for the Christmas holidays. Reverend Perry, the white manager-

---

*I felt even more strongly about the high quality of my preparation for teaching when I studied for a masters in education in the United States and found it mostly a repetition of what I had already studied.

principal of the institution, wrote that he would like to talk to me before making his final decision. He was impressed by the references I had submitted but wanted to iron out a few details before the school session began.

Soon after the New Year, 1954, I rode the family's favorite horse, Sweet Boy, to Emfundisweni to see Reverend Perry to "iron out" whatever seemed "creased" with him. After about a three-hour ride, I sat down with the reverend in his office and hoped to receive his final nod. He congratulated me on my references and expressed the hope I would join his staff when the term began in about three weeks. The only fly in the ointment was what he considered an unfavorable report from the principal of Fort Hare University stating that I was sometimes "lost in the maze of political agitation." He informed me that he personally, as a good messenger of God, did not mind Africans being involved in politics, provided they were "good" politics.

"You see, Bransby, your parents sent you to get an education to improve the lot of your people. You must not agitate against white people. I know there are some bad ones. But then there are those of us who have sacrificed everything to civilize your people. You must join with us. It took the white man a long time to get where he is. I do not want any political propaganda within the institution's grounds. Your job will be just to concentrate on educating your wards. I know at college you were exposed to all sorts of ideas about political life. I know Fort Hare in particular is full of Communists these days. We shall not have any of it here. If you promise to keep out of politics and just teach school, you've got the job. Congratulations and welcome aboard!"

I immediately stood up, took my hat and, thanking him for his fatherly advice, added, "I have a life to live right now. Our lives as Africans are controlled by the politics of the government of the day. We sleep, we dream and we even eat politics. Politics is a way of life and I find it impossible to divest myself from life itself. While I thank you for what you have said and for granting me your audience, I feel I have to hand you back the job you just offered me. Your conditions of employment are utterly unacceptable to me. Mother Africa expects much more from me than the guidelines you've just dictated. Again, I thank you, but you can gladly have your job back." I left without another work exchanged between us.

I then went to my horse and galloped him toward the trading shop a mile away to buy something to drink. The missionary had not even offered me a cup of tea. As I was about to reach the shop, I heard the priest blowing the horn of his car; apparently, he had decided to follow me. I stopped and we exchanged some words. He said, "All right, Bransby, you can come and teach as long as you do not overdo politics. It is too late for me to advertise for another history teacher now."

I replied, "Sorry, *Mfundisi* [Priest], it is too late for me not to 'overdo politics' now," and rode on, not even stopping at the shop in case he would still be following me. I wanted to avoid any further exchange of words with him, especially in public. African people really do revere and respect priests, ministers, clergymen and clergywomen representing all religious faiths. I would be the loser in African eyes if any rough exchange took place. Fortunately, he did not follow me any farther; he would not have been able to, in any case, as I changed my route to the direction of the forests where there were no roads for cars. Thus ended my endeavor to teach at the school of my parents which would have made it possible for me to spend some weekends at home.

The previous month, December 16, to be exact, I had attended a nationwide teachers' conference at Queenstown convened by the Cape African Teachers' Association. I had met many militant teachers there. One of them, R.S. Canca, who is now a practicing attorney in the Transkei, had informed me he had resigned his position as history master at Lamplough Secondary School to serve articles—an internship—as an attorney. When I got home from Emfundisweni, I immediately applied for that post.

I liked the reports I had read about the political awareness to be found in the Butterworth area. The manager of schools there, Reverend D.S. Ndubela, was one of a few black progressive priests. He replied within two weeks by telegram appointing me to the post vacated by Canca, so my teaching predicament had been solved. Now that I had a post without any strings attached, my mother helped me to celebrate the occasion by killing a fat ram, and we invited some friends to join us. We also drank from many bojanas.

In a few days I was on my way to Butterworth to teach. Though I had never met Reverend Ndubela, it was not as if I were going to a new world and other minds. I was soon to find out that one of the reasons prompting his speedy response by telegram was the fact that, when he called Professor Dent, principal of Fort Hare University, the latter started off by praising my academic achievements and then ended with "The anticlimax to all his assets is too much involvement in politics." This actually was what Reverend Ndubela, who was a Black Nationalist, considered the real climax of my education. In welcoming me on my arrival at his office, he said, "We send you as our sons to colleges so that you may change the politics of this country."

The knowledge and abilities I had acquired during my university days to do just that were to be strongly tested during my first year of teaching, which coincided with the first year of Bantu Education.

A typical southern African village.

Alan Hutchison Library

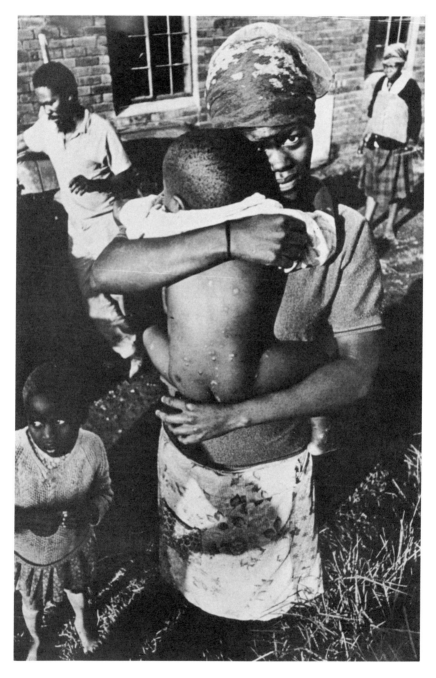

A family on a plantation in Natal owned by a British company.

An old man on one of the bantustans.

Ernest Cole

Primary schooling under the hated Bantu Education.

Tony McGrath

Black nannies in a Johannesburg park.

A segregated pedestrian bridge in Cape Town.

Some of the men who created the laws—E.M. Vorster and his Cabinet.

South African police—the enforcers.

Camera Press

Black police attacking demonstrators.

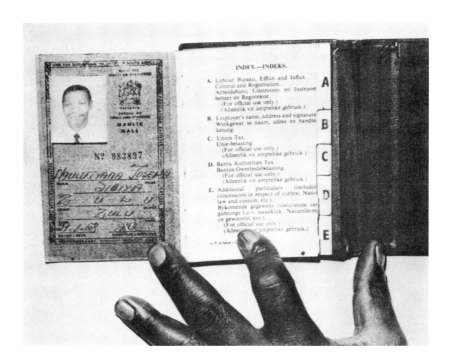

The passbook.

Ernest Cole

A pass-law offender.

Peasant women protest the issuing of passbooks to women, Transvaal, 1957.

Camera Press

A passbook burning.

A demonstration against the pass laws, Johannesburg City Hall steps, 1960.

Sharpeville, 1960—sixty-nine people shot and killed by police in a peaceful demonstration.

Robben Island prison—for political prisoners, no remission of sentence.

White student demonstrators, Johannesburg, 1972.

Tony McGrath

The future belongs to them.

All photographs are from the collection "Southern Africa—The Imprisoned Society," compiled and published by the International Defense and Aid Fund for Southern Africa as part of its work to keep the conscience of the world alive to the issues at stake. Additional sets of the exhibition, as well as many pamphlets and other publications containing information about Southern Africa, can be obtained from IDAF, 104 Newgate Street, London EC1, England.

6

Yemk'imfundo, or "Away Goes Education"

Within a month after my graduation as an educator, even before I had entered the classroom to teach at Lamplough Secondary School in Butterworth, I attended an emergency "all-in"—irrespective of race or color—conference of South African teachers in the city of Queenstown on December 16 and 17, 1953. This important conference was convened by the Cape African Teachers' Association to draw up a common strategy to fight and defeat the imposition of Bantu Education. Since Bantu Education was to be uniform throughout the country, it was necessary for the teachers' unions from each province in the then-Union of South Africa to come together to form a united front.

Each of the four provinces of South Africa—Transvaal, Orange Free State, Natal and Cape Province—had a strong teachers' union. Because of the nature of the segregated system of education, there were European associations for whites, African unions for Africans and other associations for Indians and coloreds. The white unions had nothing to do with the other unions, and their fundamental policies varied according to which white government was in power. All in all, the white unions were an appendage of the governmental system and existed mainly to maintain the status quo and spread government propaganda. The policy of the African and other non-white unions was to guard against the apartheid system's infiltration into the noble profession of education.

In the Cape Province, the most popular union and the true guardian of educational thought and learning was the Cape African Teachers' Association, which was founded in the 1920s. Its motto, "Where there is no light, the people perish," was firmly believed in by its members and adhered to in word and deed. CATA teachers pledged themselves "to bear the banner of light," to educate the people and the children under their care in goals worthy of all human beings. Another teachers' union in the Cape whose members were both colored and Indian was the Teachers' League of South Africa, founded in the 1930s. It was also a militant educational forum whose motto was "Let us live for our children." CATA and TLSA often cooperated as a federated body, especially when African and colored educations were removed from the provincial departments of education and placed under political departments dealing specifically with these two ethnic groups. The majority of black teachers belonged to these two unions.

There were two splinter organizations to which the collaborators with the government belonged: the Cape African Teachers' Union for Africans and the Teachers' Educational Professional Union for coloreds. These two were most despised by the people and were really of no concern because they dared not even have parent-teacher unions, as CATA and TLSA did. Up north in the Transvaal the most militant union was the Transvaal African Teachers' Association. There again, government collaborators formed the Transvaal African Teachers' Union, as others in Natal formed the Natal African Teachers' Union, an off-shoot from the militant Natal African Teachers' Association. So it happened that the "A" ending an organization's acronym—CATA, TATA, NATA—began to symbolize superior aims. Slogans applied to the "A" were "All-out for Above Knowledge and Progress," while slogans applying to the "U"—CATU, TATU, NATU—were interpreted as "Underlings Under the Bosses" and "Unknowledgeable with the Collaborators."

The constitution of CATA was based on emphasizing the importance of the role of teachers as custodians and guardians of the highest standards of education, teaching children and utilizing their talents to the utmost. The teachers were exhorted to be vigilant against anything that would degrade and undermine the very concepts of righteousness and progress for the general good of all. The constitution even included parts of the Ten Commandments. When the government of South Africa set up the Eiselen Commission and invited different organizations, both professional and civic, to testify, CATA and TLSA refused to do so. Both organizations could see that the government had cunningly brought the politics of apartheid into the educational system in order to defeat the equality which teachers had aspired to attain for their students as well as themselves.

Prior to the 1950s CATA, like all other white educational and professional organizations, had enjoyed recognition by the Cape Education Department. When it stood up in defense of education against the would-be miseducators, the governmental Bantu Administration Department, CATA ceased to be recognized as a professional unit of education. The Cape Education Department refused to deal with CATA on any matters of education, branding it "political," "militant" and "subversive." Yet who was politicizing and subverting African education? Who was entrenching racism? You cannot fight a bullet from a gun by throwing stones, nor do you learn to swim by studying the specific gravity of water but by jumping into the water and swimming. The government had politicized education their way and we were to politicize it our way—the people's way. We had no choice if we were to remain loyal to and uphold our convictions about the teaching profession.

With an awareness of all these circumstances, all unions were invited, and the all-in teachers conference in Queenstown drew teachers from three of the four provinces—Cape, Transvaal and Natal—with representation from CATA, TATA and NATA. A large delegation also came from TLSA. I was there as well to prepare myself as fully as possible for my first teaching job. At the opening of the meeting, messages were read from the executive committee of the Orange Free State African Teachers' Association expressing solidarity with the conference and regretting that they could not attend and agreeing to support any resolutions passed by the conference.

The Transvaal delegation was led by Zephania Mothopeng, who is presently serving a thirty-year prison sentence on Robben Island for having led the 1976 Soweto uprisings by students who opposed and agitated against Bantu Education. The Natal delegation was led by B. Gcabashe, who has also served prison sentences on Robben Island. The Cape delegation was led by the president of CATA, the late Lincoln Mkentane. He and I were among the first nine teachers in the country to refuse to sign contracts requiring pledges to uphold the tenets of Bantu Education. Prior to his death and while he was a practicing attorney in the Transkei, he also served a number of years in Robben Island Prison; there he developed the cancer that led to his untimely demise, the same set of peculiar and suspicious circumstances in that harbinger-of-death that led to the death of Mangaliso Robert Sobukwe.

In opening the conference, Kent, as Lincoln Mkentane was known among his colleagues, remarked: "Torch-bearers of the millions of our people, we are meeting here today to resolve a matter of life and death. When you cripple and poison the minds of the young, you are killing a whole nation. The enemy in the form of Bantu Education is at our doorsteps poised to deal a death blow once and for all to the education of our children. Shall we stand by with arms folded and allow this human rampage to take unchallenged its toll of our young? The people of Africa did not educate us for nought. As our motto so aptly puts it, 'Where there is no light, the people perish.' We are the light. Let us show our resolve and determination to stand for righteousness and be on the people's side to save their and our children."

He continued to speak at length, as is most usual for Africans. People on the African continent are interested in the ideas of respected leaders and will sit, listen and think for hours. Much of Kent's talk dealt with the poison of Bantu Education. He repeatedly asked teachers, "Are we going to allow ourselves to cheat humanity itself by succumbing to the dictates of racism?" Much was said in an effort to clarify misguided notions about race. He explained: "All scientists agree that there is no 'race' that is superior to another and there is no 'race' that is inferior to others. We take the view that there is only one race to which all belong, and that is the human race. In our vocabulary, therefore, the word 'race' as applied to man has no plural form. We do, however, admit the existence of observable physical differences between various groups of people, but these differences are the result of a number of factors, chief among which has been geographical isolation....

"Here in South Africa, the myth of race has been propounded and propagated by the imperialists and colonialists from Europe in order to facilitate and justify their inhuman exploitation of the indigenous people of the land. It is from this myth of race with its attendant claims of cultural superiority that the doctrine of white supremacy stems. Now you, the bearers of the light of education, are being asked to betray the trust given you by the parents to deceive and cheat their children into believing that the white man is superior—for that is what is implicit in accepting the contents of Bantu Education. As the motto of our sister organization, the Teachers' League of South Africa, so correctly puts it, 'Let us live for our children.' We have only one choice as custodians of the education of the people's children. Reject Bantu Education and fight for education that leads to the enrichment of all mankind."

Kent appealed to traditional values: "Let us meet our challenge for our children so that when we are dead they may not spit on our graves but instead proudly say of each of us, 'This was a man'!" He was much supported by the other teachers, and frequently applauded. After giving a critical analysis of the entire syllabus and structure of Bantu Education, Kent ended his speech by exhorting us to fight for what we believed was right, quoting from Claude McKay:

> *If we must die—let it not be like hogs*
> *Hunted and penned in an inglorious spot,...*
> *If we must die—oh, let us nobly die,*
> *So that our precious blood may not be shed*
> *In vain;...*
> *Like men we'll face the murderous, cowardly pack,*
> *Pressed to the wall, dying, but fighting back.*

ıt was generally resolved after two days of discussion that it would be the teachers' obligation to exorcise any kind of slave mentality in education and to impart to the African masses a sense of self-reliance that would make them choose "to starve in freedom rather than to have plenty in bondage" and prefer self-government to the alien-imposed government often preferred by moderates. We were not hoping for a change of heart on the part of the oppressor; we were reminding our people that acceptance of any indignity, any insult, any humiliation is acceptance of inferiority. We were to go out and remind our people that they must first think of themselves as men and women before. they could demand to be treated as such. The campaign against Bantu Education would free the African mind, and once the mind was free, the body would soon follow.

We were not fighting just Bantu Education or just apartheid. We as teachers were making an appeal to all other African intellectuals and businessmen, the urban and rural proletariat, to join forces in a determined war against white supremacy. We were fully aware of the nature and size of our task. There would be plenty of suffering ahead. The oppressors would never take lying down these demands and our association with the people. Some teachers would lose their jobs and others would be jailed. But the final word to the waverers and fence-sitters was "Choose now, because very soon we shall be saying with Biblical simplicity that he who is not with us is against us."

These were our resolutions and strategies to fight the poisonous education of inequality. Every teacher would be expected to join some form of community organization whose purpose would be to fight for equality in whatever way it could; we would start by giving advice to people regarding how best to fight Bantu Education—on political platforms, in civic organizations, in church centers—any place where we could be heard. We of CATA were to be the vision, the torchbearers to our people. We knew this was going against the paymasters, the government, but we owed it to a greater paymaster, the people themselves, to expose the truth and aid humanity. What a wonderful inspiration this conference was for me as a beginning teacher!*

---

*It is very interesting to note that the foundation laid down to fight Bantu

Bojana Vuyisile Jordan

The Best of Times, the Worst of Times

I was very aware of the politics involved in educational administration and decision-making, as were most African students who had attended Lovedale and Fort Hare. This only further convinced me of the necessity to build opposition to every policy with which the hated apartheid was intertwined. Yet life must be met on a day-to-day plane of individual experience and perception, so I must now filter through the overriding political concerns of the time and remember some of the more personal impressions of that first teaching year.

Although I had often traveled past Lamplough Secondary School while growing up in the Transkei, when I arrived for my teaching assignment I was more impressed than ever before by the school grounds with their beautifully decorated rows of flowers planted and cared for by teachers and students. The sweet aroma of flowers of all kinds permeated the air. Later I found out that strangers and parents alike, when passing by the school, would pause and admire the sight. Roses, tulips and all sorts of other flowers were so plentiful that at times we would invite these passers-by to pick as many flowers as they liked.

Down below the school premises and above the banks of the Cegcuana River was the school vegetable garden, where the boys worked for a few hours each day. Vegetables such as cabbage, cauliflower, carrots, beetroot, spinach, pumpkins and potatoes were grown there for the benefit of both teachers and students. Next to the vegetable garden was a vineyard and an orchard of peaches, apples, plums and other fruit trees. When schools closed for the winter or summer holidays, a man would

---

Education on those two days in December still held firm twenty-three years later when thousands of students in Soweto rose against Bantu Education. Most of them were not even born at the time we assembled.

Today the struggle continues unabated. The people are determined to win, and Bantu Education is just one line of battle. The fight is being carried on not only by the present generation but by many of those who contracted to undertake these obligations to people and country in 1953. With the murder of hundreds of school children in Soweto, with thousands of our freedom fighters languishing in jail, we know that it is the darkest hour of the morning that precedes dawn. We are at the dawn of a free South Africa which follows after the people purge the oppressive institutions of racism and exploitation. Life, liberty and the pursuit of happiness will be ours.

be hired to remain in the school solely to take care of these gardens.

The buildings comprising Lamplough were equally attractive. Their arrangement on the grounds was similar to campuses throughout Africa: a large, L-shaped, one-story framework housed most of the classrooms. Each classroom could be entered from outside without walking through other classrooms, not unlike the arrangements of many motels in the United States. The roof slanted and extended beyond the classrooms, forming a veranda area for waiting before or after classes. A large, separate hall stood to one side for use during assemblies, morning prayers, music lessons, graduation exercises, visiting speakers and a host of other activities. The setting was parklike and impressive.

After a tour of the campus, I was escorted to the area within the school grounds where the teachers' homes were located. Each teacher enjoyed either a nice rondavel or a compact, square home; some were beautifully thatched and others built of red baked bricks with corrugated iron roofs. The other three teachers, I was to discover, were married and lived with their families. As a single young man I lived in a thatched house with a bedroom, dining room, study room and a kitchen.

Though Lamplough was a missionary school, the people themselves had built the structure with their own sweat, money and materials. The missionaries mainly provided the spirit; their physical presence and prayers encouraged the people to go on with "the good work of providing a learning place for the children of God." The government provided the teachers' salaries from the taxes of the people. The missionaries were the headmasters, and the administrators who received these government checks and passed them on to the teachers. Whenever there were repairs to be made in the school, the people of the area would do them themselves, just as the students were the custodians or janitors who kept the buildings and grounds neat and clean. This was typical of all levels and grades in the Transkei, and in the country as a whole.

There were three major levels in the school: forms 1, 2 and 3 Junior Certificate, each averaging fifty to seventy-five students, thus giving the school a population of less than 250. JC 1, 2 and 3 were roughly equivalent to grades 8, 9 and 10 in the United States. It took three years for African students to graduate with a JC diploma, whereas it took white students only two years, though the syllabus, curricula and examinations were identical. The rationale for the discrepancy in the length of time to learn and prepare for the exams was that Africans took much longer to learn anything than whites. Also an extended period of time in school meant more money Africans had to pay, more dropouts because of lack of funds and, ultimately, fewer educated Africans.

All the teachers and the principal were male. Each of us had students throughout the three forms. I taught Latin in the lower form, English and history in the upper forms. This meant I always had at least 150 papers a week to correct if I gave tests only once a week; more often than not I gave more. If a teacher did his work conscientiously, as we all tried to do, he gave several written tests a week based on the assumption that the more practice a student got, the better prepared he or she would be for both exams and life. However, this meant much time devoted to corrections after school.

Classes started at 8:00 a.m. and ended at 2 p.m. The typical school day began with prayers, usually conducted by the principal himself and lasting about fifteen minutes. In his absence the teachers would rotate the responsibility. You did not have to be a Christian; it was part of your job contract since Lamplough was a missionary school. We had to attend prayers, no exceptions made.

Since there were no resident boarding masters or mistresses, it was also the teachers' duty to take care of the students after school by engaging them in one activity or another. The only time that students could be without us was when they had meals or when they went to bed at 9:00 after evening study classes. This gave us an excellent opportunity to get to know our students, both in and out of class, and afforded the chance to minister to needs of all kinds, whether study-related or personal.

Since this was my first teaching assignment, I was given the responsibility of coaching the athletic teams of the entire school. Two days a week I coached boys' soccer and rugby, and two days I coached girls' basketball. At Fort Hare I had captained the first Rugby XV team and I had been a crack sprinter in track events (100-yard, .220-yard and half-mile races). This physical exercise kept me in good condition. But as full as my day was, I didn't get to bed very early; instead, almost every night I had to prepare lesson plans, unlike the older and more experienced teachers who could rely on their lessons from previous years.

Our students ranged in age from about fourteen to twenty-two. Why this wide range for secondary school students? In South Africa African students pay for every aspect of their education, from room, board and tuition to books, clothing and uniforms. There were always more boys in class than girls, although for the population at large statistics are the other way around. Boys who wanted education badly enough usually left school after grade six and went to work to raise the money to continue with their schooling. There were many of these students in almost all of my classes, men who had returned from work in the mines, in industry and other forms of labor intent on furthering their education. Their presence was always very welcome, because they were usually so serious and intent on "getting on with the business of learning." If any of the younger students playfully distracted the attention of the class from the studies at hand, the older ones would ensure that discipline was maintained without being invited to do so. In any case, there were hardly any disciplinary problems among our students.

African students, secondary and high school, are easily the most disciplined in the world; this is my opinion after having taught school in four African countries, one European country and the United States. In fact, there is no comparison between the behavior of African and American students. African students are taught respect for their elders at home, and they accept this from the start. No African secondary or high school student, for instance, would dare smoke publicly, use profanity or even answer a teacher back. Unfortunately, that was not my experience when I went abroad. My students at Lamplough were the most pleasant group to work with by far; I still miss them today even though they have long since grown.

Students had a habit of nicknaming all their teachers according to whatever traits they liked or disliked in them. After six months at Lamplough I found out my nickname was "Mdengentonga," or "Tall by Sticks." This roughly refers to a short person with big brains. I am five-feet, three-inches tall. Perhaps they admired more what I said than what they saw according to my physical stature.

I loved all my students. I had no particular "teacher's pet," for I thought I was quite popular with all of them and did not want to spoil that by having favorites. My daily contact with the students enabled me to discuss almost all subjects affecting their lives, from religion and social conditions to politics in general. Unlike the teachers' association meetings, I could freely expatiate on the political ills of the South African system without reservation, as there were never any police to monitor my words. With the recent introduction of Bantu Education, I drove home to students that there were no pros in this situation of "Education for Slavery," no two sides to the extension of the hated apartheid system. What more could one wish for in South Africa at that time than to be given charge of the minds of youth? Indeed, I tried my best to do for them what every educator anywhere should do: develop a pansophic approach to their character development. Students should be made to know all that there is to know about life, the good and the bad, and, most importantly, how to eradicate the bad things around them. I am proud to say I spent quite some time outside the classroom talking to students about the need for revolution in South Africa by whatever means the people had at their disposal, and what it would take to create a society offering life, liberty and the pursuit of happiness for all. To me this did not feel like "teaching revolution"; it was a duty I felt incumbent upon any teacher worthy of the title. I was a teacher, not a cheater. There is nothing I have so far enjoyed more in life than being given charge of those beautiful young African minds for eighteen months. I certainly told it like it was to them and I would happily do the same again.

Students whose homes were within easy reach of the school were permitted to visit their parents. In a number of cases, when the parents arrived on Friday afternoons or Saturday mornings to pick up their children, I would also be invited to visit the homes if I could fit such a visit into my schedule. More often than not, I was delighted to accept such an opportunity. Ninety percent of the time transportation was by horseback, which I loved then and now. One or two of my students would warn me in advance that their parents would arrive with an extra horse to invite me to their homes on a weekend. It was very rare that I refused such opportunities to rub shoulders with parents and discuss national issues affecting them and their children. I tried never to visit one home twice, except in exceptional circumstances, because I wanted to exchange viewpoints with as many parents as possible.

Parent-teacher cooperation is an important ingredient of the educational system in Africa. School children do not exist in a vacuum; they are a part of the society where both the teachers and the parents live. Since teachers and parents play the most major roles in their children's lives, the two groups should share and exchange ideas on how best to supplement one another in shaping the ideals and the life of a child. A good teacher will want to know what problems the parents have with a child, if any, in order to help resolve them, and vice-versa. Therefore, parent-teacher associations are not just get-togethers but also necessary links in the educational chain.

My visits to the different homes would first concentrate on the progress and problems of the student at home and in school. Suggestions would be made as to how best each of us, teacher and parents, could interact. After this discussion I would ask to be introduced to other villagers to discuss education in general. In almost every case, we discussed the ills of Bantu Education. In South Africa you do not have to be a professional politician to talk politics. Life itself is so regimented by the politics of white superiority and black inferiority that people readily understand the position you are taking and why you are motivated to do this work.

Roughly one Saturday every other month I would accompany the sports teams when they played other secondary or high schools in the Transkei region, such as Blythswood High, Nqabara, Fort Malan, Colosa, Reiner and Tutura. After the students had finished playing in the afternoons and while they were having supper and dance parties with students of the host schools, I would have meals with the other teachers. After greetings, inquiries about friends and relatives and other polite talk, we would almost invariably settle into discussions on the political and national situation. More often than not these discussions would zero in around Bantu Education.

I had many male and female friends, or "talking acquaintances," in the villages around Butterworth, and I would visit them during weekends when I could take a few hours away from school duties. Of course, during conversations the political atmosphere in South Africa was always a good topic for discussion.

About three miles or a thirty-minute walk from our school was the Butterworth Nursing Hospital. Most of the nurses lived in the nurses quarters where visitations were allowed up to midnight. I had a lovely girlfriend, Rose Kakaza, who was a nurse there. Two or three times a week I would visit her at about 8:00 p.m. We had a standing schedule, about these visits more or less, so she would expect me at that time. I would always send a message through one of the nurses the minute I arrived at the hospital, yet despite all this I would always have to wait for at least twenty minutes before the daughter of Kakaza would appear, dressed up and ready for our date. Though I was always a little annoyed by these delays, I was never surprised. Rose lived with other nurses, and it would never do for a woman to show herself too eager to meet her sweetheart, as if she might be afraid of losing him. Oh no! She must show her independence, and that she is somebody's daughter. Rose was keenly watched by the other nurses to see if she would "grow wings" when she knew that I had arrived. There were only five of us in the whole town who were Fort Hare graduates. Educated men in South Africa were desired by many women, but if she showed excitement about me openly, others would start teasing her about hanging on to me as if they were going to snatch me away from her.

The trouble with African women is that they like to appear reserved about their love affairs. Some carry this reservation too far. Sometimes when a man offers his love, even if it is a matter of love at first sight on the woman's part, she will keep him dangling between hope and despair for the sole purpose of demonstrating to the world in general how crazy young men are about her. Some women miss out on good bachelors by following this traditional behavior; some fellows are not that patient and would just as soon pass by girls who play petty waiting games. I was on the confident side, so I did not really mind because I knew that in most cases I would win in the end. Besides, I had enough work, politically and educationally, to keep me occupied while they were pretending to make up their minds.

Rose and I dated steadily until I left Butterworth for Cape Town, and even afterwards we exchanged visits. During our time together we only briefly discussed the national political situation. Most of our conversation was about love. If you were to ask what exactly had been the subject of two lovers' conversation, they would never be able to tell you, even if they tried. In this respect Rose and I were just like any other pair of young lovers. My visits with her were such a good and relaxing change from the hard day of teaching and the rough-and-tumble of politicking.

But nearly all my weekends were devoted to organizing the people not only to oppose Bantu Education but to fight oppression on all fronts, and I often traveled dozens of miles on horseback. I became more and more active, not only in teachers' meetings but also in purely political organizations such as the Transkeian Organized Bodies, the All-African Convention and several other civic organizations whose sole aim was to undermine the status quo in South Africa.

Under these circumstances, I remained in the teaching field from January 1954 to September 1955. I was faced with the continuous challenge of grappling with the realities of what I had chosen as my calling in life. To me, education essentially meant developing the children's minds and characters, bringing out the best in them and channeling those beautiful energies to provide the most worthwhile and humane traits for society.

After all, the word "education" is derived from the Latin *ex*, meaning "out," and *ducare*, meaning "to lead." Leading the inherent good out of my charges was my basic interpretation of the word, not planting in them the poisonous seeds of racism.

Dismissal and Freedom

Meanwhile, all schooling in South Africa was feeling the brunt of the imposition of Bantu Education. The Bantu Education Department, a section under the BAD, had mobilized massive resources to take over the teaching profession and completely control the teachers. The whites in government must have understood that teachers, more than any other single group of people, determine the attitudes and shape the ideas and aspirations of a nation.

The government decreed various levels of qualifications for African teachers. The conditions of work were drastically changed. Teachers were subjected to Draconian restrictions and were always under threat of dismissal. They were expected to work under the control of the Bantu community school boards and committees, the majority of whose members were pliant and often illiterate nominees of the government. The sycophantic tribal chiefs were given the job of immediately supervising the teachers. These chiefs, who were appointed and not hereditary, had been indoctrinated to help in the weeding-out process because the teachers were, by reputation, hostile to Bantu Education and the accompanying Bantu homelands schemes which provided the chiefs with their authority.

Under the control of Bantu Education, the African teacher was humiliated, and thus his or her status in the community was drastically reduced. Teachers' salaries, based on differentiated qualifications, were scandalously low. Teachers no longer enjoyed the security of tenure or the freedom traditionally linked to the profession. One of the regulations that made it almost impossible for teachers to fight back was this: "The teacher may not contribute to the press by interview, or in any manner, or publish letters or articles criticizing or commenting on the Department of Bantu Education or any official."[11] A violation of any of the myriad regulations was punishable arbitrarily by fine and/or summary dismissal and/or imprisonment.

The same treatment was extended to African teachers in the colleges and universities. The regime took precautions to ensure that African lecturers and instructors in these colleges would not overstep their bounds. A new set of rules stipulated that African lecturers were not employed by the college councils but directly by the BED and were therefore subject to civil service regulations. They were paid substantially less than their white colleagues and were guilty of misconduct if they publicly criticized the government. A professor or lecturer was deemed guilty of misconduct if he "commented adversely upon the administration of any Department of the Government or territory of South West Africa, ... or if he propagates any idea ... calculated to impede ... the activities of any Government Department."[12]

The government promotion of Bantu Education was directed towards the parallel goal of the establishment of the bantustans in South Africa. These officially designated homelands are the Transkei, Ciskei, KwaZulu, Bophuthatswana, Lebowa, Venda, Gazankulu, Qwaqwa, KaNgwane and KwaNdebele. They comprise the reserve areas, rural territories inhabited almost entirely by Africans following traditional patterns of life. Their combined areas is nearly 60,500 square miles, which is only 12.4 percent of the total area of South Africa, or about the size of the state of Michigan in the United States.

All Africans, including those born in the urban areas of South Africa, were expected to eventually either find their way or be forced onto one of these bantustans, where they would learn "to develop along their own lines" as "separate nations." The Bantu Education system was intended to produce the trained manpower to serve the needs of these "nations." An eminent African educationist, Govan Mbeki, has described these homelands as "South Africa's backwaters, primitive rural slums, soil eroded and underdeveloped, lacking power, resources and without developed communication systems. They have no industries, and few sources of employment. They are congested and permanently distressed areas where the inhabitants live on a narrow ledge of starvation ... their chief export is labor ... their people pursue a primitive agriculture incapable of providing even subsistence."[13] The concept of the

116

bantustans provided the Afrikaner Nationalists with additional rationale that rendered Bantu Education an efficient tool of apartheid.

Bantu Education was to be geared to the perpetuation of tribalism and the pre-industrial way of life in which tribalism flourished. It was an inheritance, Dr. W.G. McConkey, former director of education in Natal Province, explained, from the days of widespread poverty and rural underemployment, when the African was seen as a competitor for the limited number of jobs available. The "tribal Native" would be good and would not compete with the white man. McConkey thought Bantu Education was the only system in the world designed to restrict the productivity of its pupils in the national economy, to keep them performing lowly and subservient tasks, to fix them mentally in a tribal world and to teach them that equality was not for them.[14] Other critics of Bantu Education described it as an instrument of creating and ensuring "the continuance of a voteless, rightless and ignorant community whose main purpose in life, apart from reproducing their kind, is to minister to the whites."[15]

There was no doubt in the minds of the majority of the people that Bantu Education was an integral part of the Afrikaner Nationalist apartheid policy. In the schools children were expected to recognize the legitimacy of the apartheid system and were obliged to use words such as "nations," "Bantu" and "homeland." The schools, thus recast, were intended to spawn tribalists who would serve the various bantustans. The meaning of terms such as "separate nations," "self-supporting Bantu communities" and "independent states" could be seen as crucial elements in the apartheid design. The emphasis on "mother tongue as medium of instruction" fitted neatly into the pattern concocted to dismember the African people into potentially warring factions that would become easy prey to perpetual domination by the Afrikaner Nationalists.

The entire diabolical scheme spilled across South Africa and, of course, into the Butterworth District where I was teaching. There were more evidences of apartheid and Bantu Education than print in this book. For example, at teachers' meetings many things could not be said because it was illegal to say them in public. If I had made a statement that suggested encouraging open revolution or mass strikes, I would have landed in jail. All teachers' meetings at this time were attended by a "special branch" of the government and the armed police. Twice in Butterworth when we held open discussions on how best to topple the racists as a whole, the police broke up the meetings because we all refused to give them the names of those who were the principal speakers or those who were "speaking up."

In early March 1955, contracts were sent out from Pretoria to all teachers in all African schools. These were to be signed and returned within three months. Among other stipulations, each teacher had to agree to teach African children according to the syllabus outlined in the Bantu Education Act. I read it with fury and disgust. I never signed nor returned mine. When schools closed for the winter vacation, I was served this notice of termination by the Bantu Administration Department:

> *Department of Bantu Education*
> *Private Bag*
> *Pretoria*
> *June 1955*
>
> *Mnumzana B.V. Jordan*
> *Lamplough Secondary School*
> *Butterworth, C.P.*
>
> *Greetings,*
>
> *You have been deemed an unfit person to teach under this Department.*
> *This is to inform you that your services under Bantu Education will be terminated on 30th September 1955.*
>
> *Greetings,*
> *Department of Bantu Education*

Notice that the letter begins with "greetings" and ends the same way, one of a million examples of the small, daily practices by whites to remind the African that he or she is an inferior and

118

must remain in the bonds of twentieth-century slavery. All employees of the BAD had been instructed never to use the salutation "Dear Sir/Madam" when writing to an African teacher, as this would recognize the African as a human being equal to whites. The administration could not countenance a black being addressed as "sir" or "madam" instead of as "servant." Nor would the usual "sincerely yours" be employed. How could an employee of the BAD be sincere to a black person?

The letter of dismissal quoted above and served on me was typical of eight others written to all leading members of the Cape African Teachers' Association. The others fired by the BAD included Leo Sinlali, the editor of the teachers' newsletter *The Vision,* who also taught at Lamplough; Lincoln "Kent" Mkentane, the president of the CATA; Nat Honono, treasurer and activist of the CATA who was then principal of Nqabara Secondary School; and two of Nat's assistants—Templeton "Major" Maja, who later became a lawyer (as did Kent and I), and Sastri Mda. By this time the students in the schools where we taught should have known all about the meaning and ramifications of Bantu Education.

We were given three months to wind up our teaching assignments. This could not have been better. We were going to "sock it to the kids," the monstrousness of this education for slavery. They now knew first hand that anyone who spoke against Bantu Education or the BAD would be summarily dealt with and punished. They saw their teachers being victimized for refusing to indoctrinate them in the ways of slavery. We intensified our agitation against Bantu Education while not neglecting to emphasize the academic aspects of the disciplines.

A week before schools closed for the spring semester, students and parents prepared a marathon farewell reception for our send-off. There, both students and parents spoke movingly on how they were not going to take this victimization lying down. Both Leo and I replied in equally moving words. After all, we now had nothing to lose by speaking our minds except the chains binding us to the murder of the innocent minds of the nation.

In my reply to the students and parents, I pointed out: "You as students have been made intellectual orphans by being deprived of the services of those teachers who cared more about your future as human beings than they did about maintaining jobs and rewards. We have proudly refused to be part of a process which seeks to return your minds to the Dark Ages. We did our duty in showing the way to enlightenment, freedom and life itself. This is a mandate given us by the African people, your parents, our real bosses. This is a duty we happily cherished and for which we were prepared to pay any cost. The truth will win. We would do it again a hundred times.

"We are happy now to continue the fight against oppression outside the classroom, in the streets and inside of your homes, where the people are. We are confident you will continue the fight from within the classrooms whilst we supplement your efforts from outside. Remember that life is now and you must shape it today in order to live as proper human beings tomorrow.

"We leave you with good tidings that as long as injustice still knocks at the doors of your homes and classrooms, so long shall we continue to haunt and harass it by whatever means possible. We shall miss your physical bodies but never forget to work even more actively for their emancipation and the revival of your spirits and souls. They can try to imprison your and our bodies but never our minds. I have no doubt in my mind you will continue to refuse to partake of or taste the poison of Bantu Education. Refuse to drink those waters of serfdom envisaged in Bantu Education."

Since the students were attentive and with me all the way, I continued to speak to them for some time about the need for them to be forever vigilant. Then I tried to arouse the parents about the same issues; they were equally responsive and appreciative of our efforts. I concluded with a cry for solidarity among all the people: "Let us all say, 'Come rain or shine, it shall not happen in our lifetime.' We are leaving the official platform of education to enter the people's education platform with the fullest assurance in our minds that you will take up the cudgel from where we left off. It is the people who are the thickest bullet-proof vests which cannot be penetrated by the enemy's bullets, be they through Bantu Education, pass laws, or any other facet of apartheid laws. Indeed, by touching our children, they have struck a rock. They have reached a point of no return. It shall not happen here."

I had done my last speechifying as a Bantu Education teacher from inside Bantu Education halls, but a lot more was still to be heard from me. Schools were recessing the following day, Friday, September 30, my last official day as a teacher. Thereafter, I was to be a "free teacher," twenty-four hours a day. I looked forward to it, but I still remember as if it were yesterday shaking hands with parents and school children, most of whom were in tears. It was quite an emotional goodbye. I was grieved at the thought that my successor might hold back some of the truth about freedom from those who had been my most important wards as far as putting the record of freedom straight.

I had totally enjoyed my eighteen months as a teacher and guardian of the minds of an up-and-coming generation of leaders. But, as all good things usually come to an end, my sojourn with that beautiful new group of students had to be ingloriously terminated by the forces embodied in the Bantu Education wing of the BAD. Now I had been liberated to do what I thought I could do best: agitating and politicizing the masses. Trevor Huddleston was to write in 1956: "The Bantu Education Act and its implementation are the beginning of a resistance movement amongst the African people; however outwardly compliant ... there burns beneath the surface a fire of fierce resentment which one day will get out of control.... Bantu Education is one of the chief instruments of a policy of racialism whose avowed aim is the establishment of an enduring white supremacy.... But it has come too late."[16] I too was on fire. Free at last, free at last—that is how I felt about my newly won freedom! I was free to preach the gospel of FREEDOM!

***

In 1955 a meeting sponsored by a parent-teacher group further revealed black sentiment toward Bantu Education. The unions had not yet been completely crushed under the harsh laws of apartheid and were still a force capable of bringing together parents, teachers and students to try to build a just, humane social order.

Returning in thought to that day of near crisis, I believe we did all we could with the resources at hand to check the imposition of a system of education that twenty-one years later would produce the uprisings in Soweto. In August 1955, when the implementation of Bantu Education was beginning, word spread throughout the Butterworth district that some teachers who had dared to oppose Education for Slavery had been dismissed. Under the auspices of the people's civic organization Iliso Lomzi, "The Eye of the People," a meeting was convened for one Saturday afternoon at Ndabakazi Village, about ten miles west of Butterworth on the way to the Kei River. Ndabakazi was a significant locality, as the name means "Great News." The meeting was attended by teachers, ministers of religion, agricultural demonstrators and all the members and ex-members of the Bunga for the entire Transkei region. Men had converged from all corners of Butterworth as well as from the adjacent districts of Ngqamakwe, Centane, Idutywa and Willowvale. Most had come on horseback, and as the horses urinated and grazed, the men lounged on the grass, lighting their pipes and exchanging tobacco while waiting for the meeting to start.

Weeks before, the CATA, of which I was regional secretary, had distributed an elaborate pamphlet written in vernacular entitled "*Yemk' imfundo* [Away Goes Education]," which strongly condemned Bantu Education. It had been read throughout the length and breadth of the Cape Province in Xhosa and Sotho, the two major people's languages in the area. The pen can be mightier than the sword, for it disseminates the ideas and emotions that make the sword leap from the scabbard and cause men to tremble. It was a matter of fighting ideas with ideas. With low voices the men talked amongst each other, reading certain lines from the pamphlet to those who could not read. Everyone was mentally girded for this meeting.

Three of us teachers from the Lamplough Secondary School had come to the meeting on horseback. The other two teachers were Leo Sihlali, who had been dismissed as "undesirable" to teach Bantu Education along with me, and Livingstone Mqotsi,

122

whose dismissal was to follow three months later. Along the way to the meeting, we crossed a car-road. There, a chief, Bikitsha, from that district, stopped to offer one of us a ride in his car so that we could "get there earlier to meet the chiefs." Bikitsha really just wanted to be seen by the people arriving with one of the opponents so he might be thought of as sympathetic to our stand. Naturally, the offer was graciously refused. All chiefs were government employees, regarded by the people to be on the government side of any issue proposed by the government. Arriving in the company of any one of them would be inviting the distrust and permanent disrespect of the people.

The meeting was presided over by Chief Monakali, who was a leading Bunga member in the district. In his opening remarks he congratulated the government for having returned the control of education back to the people and for allowing teachers to emphasize "our customs and our language." He went on extolling the virtues of "returning to real Bantu life," interrupted by several boos and shouts of "Let's hear the people's side, not the side of the *ngcotozas* [the sellouts]!" Several men had their hands up, anxious to speak. Monakali had hardly resumed his seat when one old man, Maduna from Zazulwana, sprang to his feet, blazing with anger. He exclaimed, "What's all this? Are we now today hearing a white voice though a black mouth? How can we pin our faith on chiefs like this who have literally become recordings of 'the Master's Voice'! At such a time as this, it is we who must speak—we, the old bones whose marrow they're forever sucking; we, the old maize fields from which they're forever gleaning; we, the Madunas. The irresponsible talk of the Monakalis is what has brought misfortunes upon us. Today we have no land we can call our own, and the reason lies in that very kind of talk, in those empty words, 'returning to real Bantu life.' What does the white man know about the real Bantu life to which we are supposed to return?

"Let me tell you something about these white people who have sent the Monakalis here to poison your minds, to add insult to the injury they're already inflicting on our children. When the white man came here he had only the Bible and the gun. He stole the land, kept the gun, and gave you the Bible. Can you eat the paper that binds the Bible? As if it were not enough to steal the land and starve you and your children almost to death, he now comes here through that so-called chief Monakali to ask you if he may steal your children from you through this brain-washing called Bantu Education. He wants to poison the minds of our young ones while continuing to take the wealth of our land.

"I swear by this noble land of Africa that as long as I have breath and as long as the lightning birds of your wives have not killed me, so long will no puppet of the white man like Monakali come and tell me what is good and not good for my children and my children's children. Over my dead body will any of my children be interfered with by the ever-greedy white man."

As Maduna sat down, about a dozen men jumped to their feet, all demanding to be heard. The local headman, an old man of the Tshawe clan, pleaded with them to sit down and give each man a chance to express himself. Gasela, a young militant of about thirty who had just arrived from Cape Town, where he worked in a shipyard, expressed the feelings of the others: "*Bawo* [father], it is because we were brought up to respect those gray hairs you have that we shall sit down. Otherwise, we would be tearing that Monakali quisling to pieces right in front of your eyes. Some of us may be poor because our cattle and land were stolen by the whites with the help or connivance of the stooges like that chief, but believe me, we are not poor in thinking ability. We are not poor when it means fighting for our manhood. We can fight the white intruder and his hangers-on till the last of us is buried. I'd rather be buried on my own soil, anyway, than die sunk on a ship at sea as happened to some of my forebears who were sunk on that Mendi ship during the First World War as they went to fight overseas for the white man. The enemy is here at home. We have so kindly harbored him that he now feels comfortable and safe enough to attack our children right in front of our very noses. As I said earlier, out of respect for your gray hairs we shall sit down only as long as sense is spoken regarding the education of our children."

By this time many men were loudly speaking, pointing their fingers at Monakali, some swearing at him openly, others suggesting he "be dealt with" forthwith. The chairman finally succeeded in calling the meeting to order, and quiet prevailed. He

124

then suggested that, since it was almost sunset and since tempers were running high, the meeting be adjourned until the following Saturday. Gasela again rose. "There cannot be any compromise regarding the very lives of our children. Sunset or no sunset, we are in a crisis and we shall remain here until it is solved. The only compromise is to have one of those teachers sitting over there give us advice as to what to do under these circumstances."

The chairman thanked Gasela for his composure and expressed the wish that one of the teachers speak. My colleagues decided that I should be their spokesperson, so I stood up and said, "Countrymen and my elders, indeed I honestly understand how your and our patience has been drawn to its last degree of elasticity. As you know, distinguished parents of children we teachers know, our motto is 'Where there is no light, the people perish.' The forces of darkness, as evidenced by the government's desire to dwarf our children through miseducation, seek to destroy the next generation. Thus, we are at the verge of seeing people perish.

"That is why we are here today. We are the light that is being dimmed by the racist politics of this goverment. We refuse and will continue to refuse to abdicate from the role which you sent us to schools and colleges to fulfill. Our very integrity and ability to hold high the banner of education is being assailed. We have come to you for reinforcement. You are our last resort and the only forest that can hide us from the attacks of the enemy—the government of South Africa. We refuse to hide and you must refuse to shelter us. We must all join hands today and say, 'Onward to the enemy.' Unity is strength. Though they have tried to starve us by dismissing us from our teaching jobs, one thing they can never take from us is our will and determination to fight these injustices. Education will only be equal in a society that is based on equality.

"We implore you to join political organizations if you have not done so already, organizations that fight for political equality. If there are any teachers who dare teach your children inequality as the oppressors want them to do, isolate them and ostracize them. It must be a concern and a duty of every parent to ask their children what the teacher said each day about equality of the races in this country. No parent need to have gone to school at all to examine his or her child about the concepts of equality taught at school.

"If this government wants to create committees to run Bantu Education, we should all boycott those "select" committees. Let us form our own education committees which will hire teachers who are satisfactory to us and thus force the government to pay them. It is our taxes, after all, that pay these teachers. You see, we are not racists. We still think these white people are just human beings like us, but they are misguided because they have no black people in Europe and do not understand us. We must try all means possible to make them see our position, to make them see we are just as good as they are. If this doesn't work, we will explore the next step." As I finished, many in the audience started talking to each other about the various points which had been raised. It became an active, noisy gathering.

After a brief opportunity for others to voice opinions, everyone remembered S.E.K. Mqhayi. It was customary among the AmaXhosa to have the noted poet summarize the salient points discussed and concluded at every important people's gathering. Sogoni did just that; some women wept as he spoke:

> *What kind of a nation is this today*
> *That will not raise a finger in any way*
> *When forces of darkness steal their children away?*
> *Not even baboons,*
> *Not even bitches will let be stolen away*
> *Their beloved, hard-born young ones*
> *Without a fight to death if need be.*

There still remained two specific stances towards education which had to be reconciled once and for all. Some felt a complete boycott, which would mean withdrawing the children from the schools completely, was imperative. The proponents of this view averred that the children had to be either properly educated or not educated at all. The opponents of the boycott believed that half a loaf was better than no bread at all. They suggested that children be kept in schools to be given what could be sifted out.

When the teachers were called upon to elaborate on and analyze both of these suggestions and propose the direction to be followed, we found ourselves in a rather tight corner. The boycott would mean passing on the struggle against the system to the children. What would the parents and other adults be doing against the system while we were putting the children up front as sacrificial lambs against this education? We strongly suggested that the children be kept at school, but be taught the proper education. Sifting out the chaff would imply general acceptance of the principle of Bantu Education.

Neither the parents nor the teachers' union were in any way about to compromise on this issue. We were in accord as far as rejecting inequality of any kind in the educational system. It was the duty of the people as a whole to monitor the system and make sure the old prevailed in every school. If it could be established that any teacher professed apartheid to his students, the matter would be brought before the people's tribunal, which would investigate. If the teacher was found to have furthered the ways of Bantu Education, he would be ostracized and disciplined by the people. How these were to be done was left until such an eventuality arose.

Both suggestions were unanimously adopted and became the policy to be followed from then on. A small committee of about ten people was elected to recommend steps to be taken against teachers who transgressed this resolution. The people were not going to relent. They were not going to compromise. They were not going to equivocate. It would be the people's will or nothing at all.

As we left the meeting, the words of the poet S.E.K. Mqhayi traveled with us: *"Godukani ningalali, eyona mfazwe mna ndithi ifikile* [Go home and don't sleep, for verily I say unto you, the real war is imminent]."

7

Cape Town—A Lawyer Confronts the Law

The Transkei was familiar ground for me since I had grown up there herding cattle and traveling to night school. Because of this, and because of my position as regional secretary of the CATA, I already had many contacts with different people's groups. An extensive political tour of the Transkei region, agitating against the government's apartheid system in general and against Bantu Education in particular, was my full schedule for the first two weeks after my dismissal from the classroom. I successfully shuttled from one civic or community organization to the next. The response from the people was very positive. War against the governmental institutions that carried out the apartheid policy was declared almost everywhere I went. The questions regarding the use of varying tactics of opposition according to the issues affecting a particular locality were explored in depth.

After this campaign throughout most of Transkei proper, I headed for the city of Cape Town to find a job. On my way by train, I disembarked for half a day at the city of Alice and went to Fort Hare University to bid farewell to some friends who were still there, such as Dr. Sam Guma, who was a lecturer at Fort Hare and is now president of Swaziland University. In the evening I once again climbed aboard the train, which was routed through Port Elizabeth to Cape Town.

Before reaching Port Elizabeth the train went through the Albany District of the Cape Province, where the cities of Grahamstown and Bathurst are located. This area was settled by the British back in the early 1800s. I never thought I would become acquainted with another Albany, thousands of miles away in New York State in the United States. Port Elizabeth was the next large city, well-known as the most central of the four large South African ports.* Large amounts of wool are exported from its harbor, wool obtained from the goats and sheep bred on the surrounding *karroos*, or treeless uplands. As the train sped along the southern shore of the Cape Province I had glimpses of the beautiful blooming flowers that earned this section the title "the Garden Route." From East London through Port Elizabeth and all the way to Mossel Bay, a distance of over three hundred miles, the route was dotted with seaside resorts on one side and scattered forests on the other. Vacationers, especially from the inland provinces of the Transvaal and the Orange Free State, were eager to come here to see the beauty of the seaside areas and smell the balmy air.

By the following afternoon, after a train ride of over thirty-six hours, I arrived in Cape Town. I knew the city well, having spent most Christmas holidays there with my uncle and his family. It was rather ironic that I should look forward so much to life in Cape Town after my great disappointment with the state of affairs in the country that led to my expulsion from teaching. But I anticipated with great pleasure the renewal of old friendship, especially those formed from the Unity Movement. These leaders included I.B. Tabata, Dr. Goolam Gool, Bennie Kies, Ali Fataar, and of course, my uncle A.C. Jordan. I owed a lot to them for my political upbringing while I had been at Fort Hare University. I hoped to rejoin the friends I had made at the bi-weekly Marxist study groups I had regularly attended during my summer holidays, and I looked forward to meeting other ex-Fort Harians in the city and playing some rugby for my club, the Bush Bucks.

---

*The ports are Cape Town, Durban, Port Elizabeth and East London. The South African government also includes a fifth port: Walvis Bay in Namibia.

This journey did not feel to me like any previous one. I had spent all my Christmas holidays in Cape Town, but those occasions had simply meant vacationing and working for some college pocket money. This time Cape Town was a home where I was to make a living—a new start in life away from the classroom. I sat on the train recalling all my previous impressions and images of Cape Town, realizing my new perspective, and even thinking of its long history.

Cape Town's position where the Indian and Atlantic Oceans meet is not only majestically beautiful but of great strategic importance to all countries of the world. As the second largest city and the first exporting port of South Africa, it is often referred to as the "Tavern of the Seas." Catering to ships is an old story in Cape Town. In 1486 the Portuguese sought spices from the East and had dispatched Bartolemew Diaz to find a sea route to India via Africa. Nature was not too kind to him and his men when his two ships reached the southernmost shores of Africa. This was around November, a rather stormy season in the Mediterranean region of the Cape. Diaz's ships were buffeted, tangled and almost engulfed by the violent seas. The unsophisticated Portuguese sailors had not anticipated the state of the weather in this strategic part of the world. All they knew was that the world might be round; they could not guess at which point this might be proven. They certainly were not aware that the Atlantic and Indian Oceans clashed at this very point.

The angry storms vomited them into the mainland Cape. After a few days' rest and the food provided through the hospitality of the kindly natives, the crew was home-bound to Lisbon to report their findings to King John II of Portugal. They suggested to him that this part of the world be known as the Cape of Storms because of the bitter experience they had had. King John was so hopeful of ultimately reaching India via the Cape that he named it instead the Cape of Good Hope. My beloved home province, including the city of Cape Town and the territory of the Transkei, still goes under that exploratory and imperial name—the Province of the Cape of Good Hope.

Diaz was followed by other European voyagers, including an Englishman, Sir Francis Drake. This Englishman gave testimony to the idea that a thing of beauty can be a joy forever when, after sailing around the globe in 1580, he described the area around Cape Town as "the fairest Cape we saw in the whole circumference of the earth." To further confirm its beauty and splendor, another European, Mellville Charter, wrote from Washington DC in 1931: "Cape of Good Hope: The Floral Province. The land smell! Luckless is the ocean voyager who has missed that memorable hour when month-long, briny breezes suddenly drop and there steals upon him from afar that indescribable earth odor, breathing of imminent shores and journey's end. It greeted us and our ship one dazzling September morning. South Africa at last! We are nearing the continent which Pliny so intriguingly characterized as the source of 'always something new'."[17]

The testimonies of these three Europeans living centuries apart speak volumes. The Europeans who saw the beautiful Cape in all its majesty just refused to pass by. In 1652 Jan van Riebeck, a surgeon in the Dutch East India Company, brought a small colony of settlers to the Cape to grow vegetables for the scurvy-ridden crews of tiny vessels making the long voyage to India and the Orient, where spices and other condiments were collected and traded back in Europe for fabulous sums of money.

After van Riebeck's inauspicious settlement, more and more Europeans lay seige to southern Africa. They stayed, they stole from it, they raped it, they plundered it, they used it as a gateway into the riches of inland Africa. From the tip of Africa, white settlers found their way to the four provinces of South Africa. From all over South Africa they penetrated the whole of southern Africa, the nations of Botswana, Zimbabwe, Angola, Mozambique, Zambia and Namibia.

Cape Town, like the country itself, had become the center of industries developed from the products of the mines and farms of South Africa: for example, the processing and canning of fruit and vegetables and the manufacturing associated with tobacco, wheat, beer and cement. African wines had become internationally recognized. To the north, the plentiful coal and iron ore led to the iron and steel industries, the products of which included everything from nuts and bolts to mining and agricultural machinery, railway coaches and bicycles. All this wealth which the white minority greedily culled to themselves was built upon the blood, sweat and enslavement of the black majority who were left with no land, no wealth, no homes, no human rights, no vote—nothing but poverty and misery.

In those days I refused to allow the horrendous implications of history to defeat me. The magnificent setting of Cape Town was still able to compete with the historical injustices in my mind. The blue of the sky and the ocean, the brilliant flowers, the sub-tropical air seemed to caress me. I remembered the foliage, the red tile roofs, the outlying beaches. Once again, I saw Table Mountain jutting up from the ocean, its solid mass standing in relief against the sky and water, as flat-topped as a table. It was a great sport to climb the mountain or scale it by cable car. But apartheid was even in the cable car—blacks were seated on one side of the car; the other side was reserved for whites.

Just about a mile from Simonstown, a suburb of Cape Town, is the Cape Point. From five yards away, you can throw a stone into either ocean—this is the only point in the world where these two gigantic oceans meet. And what a gorgeous meeting it is! The upward splash when those green waters collide would challenge any poet to improve on Wordsworth: "Earth has nothing more fair to show."

I disembarked from the train, left the railway station and found myself on Adderley Street, home to tall insurance offices, the O.K. Bazaar, publishing houses, a fifteen-story post office, the big City Hall and corner flowerstands. Yes, I was back in Cape Town, with its segregated restaurants, segregated motion picture houses, segregated double-decked trams, segregated buses and segregated electric trains. Here I saw the imposing homes of the wealthy whites and the worst slums in the world for the non-whites. Many of the places where people of color lived could hardly be called houses; they were crumbling shacks of cardboard, odd pieces of wood, rusty corrugated iron and any other scraps which people could put together. Most "houses" had no toilet facilities or running water. Dr. D.F. Malan, former

Nationalist Party leader and prime minister, stated in 1953 that "The Negro does not need a home. He can sleep under a tree."*

The unusual variety of people and races was quite different from what I had been used to in the Transkei. In the region of my birth the vast majority of the people were black Africans who proudly passed on their culture to their children. Unlike the rest of the country, where coloreds were a tiny minority, in Cape Town three-fifths of the population were coloreds and Asians. These Cape coloreds were descendants of the first Malays brought into South Africa by the Dutch East India Company and had become interbred with the KhoiKohn, the black Africans, and the white settlers. Thus, the white settlers represented only a fifth of the population in Cape Town. Also found in the Cape were red-fezzed men and veiled women of Malay, who were generally Islamic and remained to themselves. The Indian group, called Asians, were often Hindu merchants and traders. The strictly black population was definitely in the minority, comprising the remaining one fifth.

I was pleased to be met at the station by many friends and members of my family. My uncle A.C. and his two sons, Lindi, and Pallo shook hands with me and asked about the journey. All my thoughts from the train ride could hardly be expressed in so little time with such a number of people making polite inquiries. Time would tell whether my thoughts about Cape Town were to be useful in building a new life for me in this city of contrasts.

From Schoolteacher to Houseboy-Gardner

My main purpose in choosing Cape Town as my new home was to continue with my political study groups, political agitation and, of course, with university studies. This time I intended to go to law school. I had known since school days that it was a crime by white law to be born black in South Africa; hence, I had no hesitation in choosing law as my next course of study. Since I had to be articled, or interned, to a law firm in order to be admitted as an attorney in South African lower courts, I

---

*This is the same Malan who during World War II made no secret of his desire that Hitler win the war.

started an immediate hunt for a law firm that would article me. Of all the law firms in Cape Town, 99.8 percent were white, so I knew it would be a tough job to find a firm liberal enough to take me. In the meantime, I had to find some kind of a job.

I landed a job as a houseboy-gardener with a Dr. Castle, a medical doctor in the white suburban area of Wynberg. The average white family had two servants, a "boy" and a maid. Since whites were paid twenty times more than blacks, they have an incredibly high standard of living; every white in South Africa can afford at least one servant.

I was a stay-in servant. Every morning I got up at about 5:30 and warmed water to wash the family dog. Then I walked the dog for about an hour and returned so that the dog and myself could have breakfast. While the maid fed the dog a fried steak and porridge with milk, I quickly took a bath and then had my own breakfast: dry bread, black coffee and porridge without milk. There was only enough steak for the dog. I then cleaned and polished the two-story house.

At about midday I had a fifteen-minute break. Then I worked in the garden until lunchtime, about 2:00. At least 60 percent of the white homes in Cape Town have vegetable and flower gardens; the Mediterranean climate is so perfect that vegetation is green for about nine months of the year. Most whites grow their own vegetables and flowers using cheap black labor. My lunch and supper meals were much better than breakfast. Whatever was left from the boss's table, or from his plate, which usually included some meat or bones, would be available for me. Lunch lasted for about an hour, after which I would go back to work in the garden till sunset. Hours of work were determined by the rising and setting of the sun. I was not paid hourly nor by the amount of work I did. I was paid a flat rate equivalent of about two dollars a week. I worked for Dr. Castle for only one week.

Why had I chosen to work as a houseboy-gardener? Were jobs that scarce for blacks in Cape Town? At the time, not really. I had worked during summer vacations for department stores like the O.K. Bazaar and Markam's, but I had heard from many black men how badly they were treated in their positions and I wanted to know at first hand how the white women treated "boys." I deliberately had not told my uncle the kind of job I had taken.

On the Saturday of my first week he drove to Dr. Castle's to deliver a message to me that we would have to attend a rally on Bantu Education that evening at Kayamandi, a black location in Stellenbosch outside Cape Town. It was blazing hot that day and I was dripping with sweat as I knelt to polish the veranda steps. My uncle's arrival coincided with the arrival of Dr. Castle, who slammed his car door and rushed over to me saying, "Boy, quickly unload the groceries from the boot of my car as I have to rush back to surgery."

I stood up and was about to do as I had been ordered when my uncle angrily confronted him. "Why can't you do it yourself? Don't you see he is sweating like a slave in that heat, polishing your veranda?"

"So what! Does he not get paid for it?" retorted Dr. Castle.

My uncle could not contain his anger. He simply said, "Boji, take your coat. Let's go. Leave this slavedriver."

I replied, "I'll have to get my week's pay first."

Dr. Castle reached into his back pocket and pulled out two pounds, about $3.50, and threw it at me, saying, "You can keep the change. I do not want to be arguing with natives." When two or more black males argue with a white man, let alone confront him, the man seems to visualize an army of blacks and becomes mortally scared. I simply said, "Alright, *Bawokazi* [Uncle], let us go," and we left. Dr. Castle could have called the police and manufactured any story—such as saying we had threatened him—and his statement would have been enough to send both my uncle and me to jail for the night. The police invariably believed what a white said about a black.

My uncle, who is now deceased, could not stand any kind of injustice from whatever source. In one of his poems, he wrote:

> *You tell me to sit quiet when robbed of my manhood,*
> *With nowhere to live and nought to call my own,*
> *Now coming, now going, wandering and wanting,*
> *No life in my home save the drone of the beetle!*
> *Go tell the worker bees*
> *True guards of the hive,*

Not to sting the rash hunter
Who grabs at their combs.

He could not stand quietly by and watch me ordered from one menial job to another. In any case, I had tasted enough of what it was like to work as a houseboy-gardener. I now would be able to describe from practical experience the ignominious role of a black servant in South Africa.

Another humiliating, unforgettable experience that I had in Cape Town was my first arrest by the police for a passbook violation. One hot summer afternoon in December 1958, I was visiting with friends in Athlone Township, Cape Town. Halfway through our discussion I had to go to the outhouse about fifty yards away, the usual distance in that part of Athlone. I left my jacket, which contained my pass, hanging on the chair because I was only going to be gone for a couple of minutes. On my way back two policemen, who had been raiding the house next door, stopped me and demanded my pass. When I told them it was in the house just ten yards away, they said, "You should know better. You ought to have your pass on your person at all times."

No amount of pleading with them to give me less than five minutes to produce it helped. They promptly arrested me and drove me to the police station to be charged with "failure to produce passbook on demand by police." I was locked up for the night pending appearance in court the following day. When my friends followed me to the police station that same afternoon to produce my passbook, they were told, "Too late, he should have had it on demand. Take it to court tomorrow morning." When I explained to the magistrate just what had happened the previous day and presented my pass, he delivered his judgment: "Accused found guilty, cautioned and discharged."

The passbook is no ordinary identification card; rather, it is a fifty-three-page book, the size of an ordinary passport, that every African has to carry on his/her person twenty-four hours a day. This is issued at the time an African reaches the age of sixteen; he/she must line up at the Bantu Administration Office to obtain this pass. The police may demand that any African produce this "pass" at any time of the day, at any place, under any circumstances, even the most inconceivable or unimaginable ones. A black must humbly subject him or herself to this afront or be arrested immediately.

These notorious passbooks are sometimes called Dom passes after settler Prime Minister G.J. Strydom. Although the first pass law goes back to 1760, it was during Strydom's reign in 1950 that the passbook become the law of the land. The government has often called it a "reference book," for all the minute details of one's life history must be listed: place of work, place of domicile, number of arrests, chief's name in the bantustans (even if one has never lived in the bantustans), paid or unpaid poll taxes, permission from the white boss (if given) to be in the streets after 9:00 p.m. or to be in a white area at all (e.g., you may not visit a girlfriend working in a white area without such permission), plus a myriad of other personal details about one's life. Failure to have listed any of these particulars or failure to have any item correctly stated renders one subject to immediate arrest.

The passbook system is one of the most diabolical of the thousands of pieces of legislation that keep apartheid in position in South Africa. The beginnings of the system go back hundreds of years when whites had all sorts of pieces of paper they gave to African employees in regard to residence, curfews or other restrictions under which Africans were subject. The pass laws are very complex. The legal position of Africans is so weak that police can arrest any black person anywhere at any time of the day or night by claiming the black has violated the pass system. Under the "legal" system in South Africa the government's prosecutor has no trouble finding some offense with which to charge blacks. Each year there are millions of arrests and convictions for violations of pass laws.

The pass laws are necessary for apartheid to function successfully, since this is one of the principal ways the mobility of blacks is checked. No African can move freely nor even apply, let alone work, at any job of his choosing.* Without special per-

---

*Even more laws establish and regulate job categories so that blacks may only be emloyed in the lowest levels. No black may ever attain a position above whites; this is legally stated and enforced.

mission he must stay employed where he is. Any black or "native" may be forcibly moved from one area to another by administrative order. Likewise whole tribes have been moved.[18] The cornerstone of these policies is the pass law system. Africans are denied all recourse to fight these injustices, peacefully or forcibly, since they are also deprived of all *human* rights.

I had a couple of other jobs before I started attending law classes at the University of Cape Town. One job I enjoyed was in the Department of Bantu Languages at the University, where I helped teach the Nguni group of African languages (Xhosa and Zulu). I also became involved in a number of other interesting activities. Weekends were mostly occupied with attending all sorts of meetings: civic association gatherings, political rallies, and study groups in the evenings. Two study groups in particular fascinated me; conducted by the New Era Fellowship and the Society of Young Africa, they were dynamic Marxist study groups examining those aspects of Marxism-Leninism that applied to the South African situation. If I was not involved with one of these study groups, I would be at parent-teacher organizations or Iliso Lomzi. I loved the activity and the involvement.

The blacks around Cape Town were about the most informed of all South African blacks because of what is usually referred to as "the Cape liberal spirit." The libraries and other cultural agencies were not totally segregated. Because ships sailing to all parts of the world went around Cape Town, the South African authorities tried to keep the city a model of race relations. Story has it that when Leon Trotsky fled Russia for Latin America, he stopped in Cape Town for a few weeks and conferred with some intellectuals across the color line. When I was there in the early fifties, Trotsky was about the most popular foreign theoretician among the black elite. The most active non-white political organizations at the time, the Anti-Colored Affairs Department (fighting against the Colored Affairs Department) for coloreds and the All-African Convention for Africans (both organizations that later federated into the Non-European Unity Movement), were all essentially Trotskyite. The leading members of these organizations, men such as I.B. Tabata of the

AAC or Dr. Goolam Gool of the Anti-CAD were Trotskyite and were unadulterated Marxist-Leninists as well.

I had a lot of fun in the township playing rugby for the Bush Bucks. Most Saturday and Sunday afternoons I spent at the Langa Sports Stadium when I was not campaigning and organizing out of town. In winter I was always involved with sports, whether playing or officiating at rugby games, and in summer I loved to watch cricket. These afternoons afforded our black sisters their only chance to change from work uniforms into ordinary clothes. Most African women worked for whites as housemaids six-and-a-half days a week. In Cape Town a few black women had longer weekends, when they could visit their families and relatives on Saturday afternoons but would be due back Sunday nights. This was the only time that white employers spent with their children, driving away to hotels or restaurants for the weekend. Otherwise, the children were completely cared for by African servants, who bathed, fed and escorted them to and from school. South African maids work from 5:00 a.m. until about 11:00 p.m. with very few breaks—all this for no more than about ten dollars a month. Very few whites, if any, ever cook or clean for themselves in South Africa.

My other regular haunts in the townships were the *shebeens*, or speakeasies, places that sold liquor illegally, especially after hours. Africans were not allowed to possess liquor of any kind unless they had received special permission. Any amount was obtainable, however, from the "shebeen queens," as the unlicensed women sellers were known. I frequented these places not so much to drink as to meet other men. A lot of political discussions, national or international, went on, and many a plot or scheme to try to topple the government was hatched.

I was always busy in Cape Town. Between the political and community involvement and the enjoyment of the beauty of the people and the environment, there was never a dull moment. But part-time and temporary jobs were soon to give way to full-time studies in law.

Entering Law School and the Practice of Law

Uppermost in my mind was finding the first available spot to apprentice as a lawyer in one of the numerous law firms in Cape Town. There was not a single black or colored firm among the hundreds in the city, and of the hundreds of law students who were articled with law firms, only two were Africans, employed by two Jewish law firms. Jewish lawyers were more sympathetic to the African cause of liberation than their counterparts.

After waiting for a long time, I was finally articled to the prestigious English law firm of Rose-Innes and Jordan right in the center of Cape Town. As articled clerks, law candidates worked in law offices from 9:00 a.m. to 5:00 p.m. and were coached in how to handle all kinds of litigation. Also, each candidate had to be registered as a full-time evening student with the University of Cape Town Law School. Classes were conducted every evening and some Saturday mornings at Hidding Hall. I duly registered and attended all the relevant law classes.

As a college graduate, my course of study was to last three full years. After the completion of the first eighteen months of internship and after passing half of the required courses, an articled clerk was entitled to appear in the lower courts to defend any case. During my first eighteen months, I attended law classes in the evenings and went to court with my principal, a senior lawyer in the firm, and listened, watched and learned.

Black students represented about 2 percent of the total student body of the law school—the case almost throughout the country—in a country where 87 percent of the population was black! Only a few other white universities took a minimal number of black students: the Universities of Witwatersrand, Natal and Rhodes. None of the Afrikaans universities (Pretoria, Bloemfontein, Stellenbosch) would dare take any black students because of their belief in carrying out apartheid in every institution and in every possible situation. Any blacks seen around those campuses were working and cleaning during the daytime; between dusk and dawn they had to be out of sight and off the university campus.

I enjoyed being in law school and studying how the South African legal system worked, especially when it came to statutory laws, most of which were specifically made against the black man. Since there were only a few of us who were black, we were at times the center of attraction for the white students. UCT was a "liberal" university, so the white students went out of their way to be kind and helpful to us. The Jewish students in particular were the most considerate. While we appreciated whatever they were trying to do, we were not about to be swayed one way or the other by any paternalistic attitudes. No doubt somebody had to make up for the white guilt of the generations who had heaped abuses on the Africans. Our business-as-usual policy was to study law, and we were not really interested in reparations by a few whites to a few "privileged" blacks.

Halfway through my law studies and the period of serving articles, around September 1959, I was sworn in by the Supreme Court and allowed to defend cases in the lower courts. By this time I had passed most of the law courses I needed for court appearances: Criminal Law, Roman Dutch Law (Law of Persons and Marriage, Property Law), Elements of Roman Law, Native Law, Conveyancing and Negotiable Instruments. All the major criminal cases for Africans were heard either in the Cape Town or Wynberg courts. Cases of civil disputes between Africans were heard in the Native Affairs Department, Salt River. All the cases pertaining to pass laws were heard before a native commissioner in Langa. Most of my time was spent in criminal and pass law cases.

I quickly became one of the busiest young articled clerks in the city. Our law firm was inundated with more court cases involving Africans than we could handle—not because our lawyers were superior to others, but because of my presence in the law firm. I was black, very much involved in community affairs, and could now appear in court. Most vivid in my memories of this period is the hopelessness and helplessness of some trial cases.

In defending criminal cases, I made a thorough study of all criminal laws and presented each case with vigor. Criminal law in South Africa is supposed to be applied equally to everyone,

142

black or white, but the net results are different for blacks. I had little problem in defending criminal cases. Naturally, I put more preparation into my cases than a white attorney would, knowing that I would have to face an all-white establishment in the court: the magistrate, the prosecutor, the court clerks and the court police officials. Black policemen were only used outside the courtroom to do all the arresting and to minimize noise. The only other black face in court would be my client's, and perhaps those of his or her relatives.

The most depressing and frustrating court cases were those involving passes, often heard in the Langa Court. Sometimes when the police raided African homes at 3:00 a.m. and the person found sleeping did not have his or her pass within easy reach—maybe it was in the closet in the next room—that person was immediately arrested. There could be no defense, because the law specifically stated that the passbook had to be carried by all Africans "at all times, twenty-four hours of the day."

Concerning trespassing and vagrancy, an African was not supposed to visit a home in a white area without a white person's permission. Even if a black person received a telephone message that a relative working in a white area was sick or injured and proceeded to visit that relative without taking time to get some kind of permission, the person ran the risk of being arrested. If the eldest child in a black home found that there was no food in the house, as was frequently the case, and he or she went to where the mother worked to get money or food for the other children, the child stood a good chance of being arrested if the police found him or her before the mother was reached. If a man decided to visit a female friend out in the suburbs without permission and was caught by the police, he had broken the law.

Very little, if anything, could be done to defend the above cases. About the best I could ever do was to plead with the magistrate or officer conducting the case to take into account the extenuating circumstances that led to the defendant's arrest. Of course, the best my client and I could even hope for was either a suspended sentence or a fine. In most of these cases my clients had to serve jail sentences since they simply had no money. In retrospect, all the lunacy of these laws becomes apparent. When you want to visit your lover, who in a normal, sober society must give you permission to do so except yourself and your conscience? And when a child is hungry, who else must the child turn to except the mother, for all ages and in all places throughout the world? Only in South Africa is a normal reaction to a situation considered abnormal. As a result, South Africa itself is an abnormality among the nations of the world.

Yet even more disheartening were the passbook cases where Africans who arrived in Cape Town illegally to look for work and were "endorsed out." If an African was in the Cape Town area to look for work without written permission from some white authority and was caught within seventy-two hours or even after that period, he was immediately endorsed out—sent back to the area from which he came. The Africans referred to this act as *Phum'aphele,* or "Get out completely." Most Africans went to the cities without these permits hoping that a friend or relative would arrange things for them when they got there, which occurred in about 75 percent of the cases.

What was so tragic and painful about being sent back home without a day's work is that the deportee was being sent back to the barren land which he left because his eyes could not bear the sight of the starvation and ill-health of his children. His ears could not bear their cries, nor the mumbling and complaining of the helpless mother about the plight of her children. He was being sent home without a penny in his pocket, and usually, he had either borrowed money from neighbors or sold his last goat or ox for his fare to the city to look for employment. Where would he get enough courage to face again all the hardship he had just left?

It is this naked, brutal injustice to the black worker in the South African cities that creates potential criminals. What else is a man supposed to do to feed his starving, dying children when he is not allowed to look for employment? Will he not try to get money by whatever other means possible? The apartheid system forces the most law-abiding people and the most willing workers to become criminals. I appeared in the Langa courtroom several times to present cases for these deportees. The law was clear cut: they had to be endorsed out. The best I could win was a "stay of the endorsement order pending looking into other avenues of relief within the law"—and in most cases there were none. Today this situation has gone from bad to worse. The surprising thing is not that there has been no violent explosion on the part of blacks against the system, but that such an explosion is taking so long to erupt. If and when it does—and the clock is ticking fast—I grieve to imagine who or what will be left, black or white. God forbid!

I remember cases in which I used to expose the foolishness of those who had to maintain the apartheid system. Let me explain the case of a sit-in protest. Two black students attended an "all-white" concert in a Cape Town hall and sat at the back by themselves. They were arrested and charged with violating the Separate Amenities Act which states that whites and blacks may not attend the same social functions in the same place at the same time. I explained to the magistrate the unconstitutionality and unreasonableness of the prosecution's case, pointing out that my clients had indeed segregated themselves by sitting alone at the back of the hall. They had had absolutely no contact with the white audience; they could not even be seen because they were behind everyone else. In this manner, I averred, my clients had practically and in spirit abided with the Separate Amenities Act.

The prosecutor jumped up to oppose my technical motion for dismissal of the case. He pointed out that what the "honorable lawmakers" had envisaged in the spirit of the law separating the two races was fundamental. He went on: "Whites cannot see a performance properly nor hear and enjoy music to the fullest as long as there are black faces around or in close proximity." These are some of the examples of the immeasurable ignorance that drives racist South Africans to extremes of madness whenever they deal with blacks.

In another case, a black university male student was criminally charged for kissing a white female student who was a friend. The two had just met in the school corridors for the first time after the Christmas holidays. When they kissed each other on the cheek, the security police arrested the black student and charged him under the Immorality Act, a law which bars any kind of physical contact between a black male and a white female. When I pleaded for mitigation and a suspended sentence before the magistrate since the kiss was a mutual agreement between the two, the magistrate said he would sentence the black male to three months at hard labor since he showed no remorse for having "dared" kiss a white person. "Kissing may lead to something else," he concluded.

I had a good number of clients among the unemployed youth, who were generally known as *tsotsis,* or "take-it-easy" types. These fellows did quite a bit of "liberating" of property from rich white homes and factories. Before going on such escapades, which the law enforcement officers called robbing or stealing, they would telephone me and tell me to expect some agent of theirs to deposit some money with me for bail and as a retainer in case anything happened to them. I would then be able to arrange for their bail and defense in case they were disturbed in their attempts at liberation. Only in very few instances were these enterprising young men caught, but in such an eventuality, I paid their bail and defended them, often quite successfully. A system that feeds on starvation through low wages and unemployment cannot be surprised when its victims manipulate the same system for their survival.

Sometimes the practice of law could be fascinating as well as helpful to the common people. Before Christ was born, the Roman poet Pliny wrote, *"Ex Africa semper aliquid novi,"* or "Out of Africa, there is always something new." Perhaps he did not have in mind the small seaport called Walvis Bay, north of Cape Town on the Atlantic Ocean. Most of the few Africans who live there work as housemaids and garden boys for the whites who tend the passing ships. Both South Africa and Namibia claim Walvis Bay, considered to be the best port on the southwestern coast, although it is located inside Namibian territory. There is no known industry there except fishing and accommodating passing ships with their cargoes. There is a credible theory, though, that around Walvis Bay quite a sizeable amount of small shining pebbles known as diamonds can be found.

In September 1959 our law firm was retained to represent two men accused of murder in what was called a civil disturbance in some compound in Walvis Bay. The state's case for the prosecution was very weak, and we were able to have our men acquitted in the preparatory stage of the examination of the case. We were in court for two days and should normally have charged an equivalent of about two hundred dollars; our clients were destitute, so we settled for anything they could offer apart from our gasoline expenses. The wives of the defendants called me aside and told me that they had hunted for what looked like diamonds on the sand just at the edge of the ocean. After taking me to their house, they showed me five of the stones. These stones looked good enough to pass for the diamonds I had seen displayed in windows of jewelry stores in Cape Town. The senior member of my law firm who had come up with me was also satisfied about their authenticity. When we returned to Cape Town, our agent disposed of them. We had enough money to buy me a 1957 Volkswagen, only two years old. In fairness to our clients and in accordance with what we considered to be ethical conduct on our part, we wrote our clients to inform them that they could retain us as their lawyers without further charge for the next twelve months. Indeed, early in 1960 we were back in Walvis Bay for a passbook offense case. This time there was very little we could do except, as usual, plead for leniency and that our clients be given a few extra months to wind up their business before being endorsed out of the city.

The land and country of the black people was taken from them over three hundred years ago. They have no civil rights. For being human they are jailed, beaten or even killed. Their only crime is being black. As a lawyer I sometimes felt like a medical doctor trying to cure an incurable disease. That disease, apartheid, has to be cut out if black people are to be saved.

A Visit to the South African Parliament

South Africa has no single capital city like most countries of the world; three specific cities have Capital importance. Cape Town is the Legislative Capital; Pretoria, the Administrative Capital; and Bloemfontein is often referred to as the Judicial Capital because it holds the Supreme Court, the highest and final court of appeal for the land. The all-white legislative body meets for six months in Cape Town, where it makes laws for whites and conspires against all blacks. The remaining six months the administrators gather in Pretoria to see to it that the laws are carried out. Meanwhile, throughout the year the Supreme Court hears all appeals in Bloemfontein. Of course, 90 percent of all cases have to do with blacks, usually concerning the death sentence or life imprisonment. Most of these are political, since opposing white domination in South Africa even by organizing people peacefully is regarded as treason and punishable by death.

While I was in Cape Town I visited the House of Assembly to hear parliamentary debates whenever I could squeeze in some time during the afternoon. Some of my friends from college who taught at Langa High School would come to my office and ask me to accompany them to Parliament. I was one of the few privileged to be issued a pass to enter the spectators' gallery because (1) I was a well-dressed "native" and (2) a senior member of my law firm was a former assemblyman and then a senator. So I had the necessary credentials to listen and learn the law-making process from the "best brains in the country."

When we visited the Houses of Parliament, we did so out of sheer curiosity. We wanted to see for ourselves what was really happening inside those securely guarded gates. Both the Assembly and the Senate Houses had the tightest security, around the clock. Nobody entered the houses of Parliament without a thorough and intensive check. When Dr. Verwoerd, prime minister of South Africa, was stabbed to death inside Parliament in 1963, the job was done by an insider, a page who was a regular worker inside the House and therefore above suspicion.

When we entered the Assembly, the processing was even more thorough. We were searched for weapons, knives and guns. No newspapers or scratch pads were allowed into the gallery. As spectators we had to be dead silent. Before the debates started, we could hear a pin drop, but once the actors on the lower floor of the General Assembly started making laws for themselves and against "the people" (blacks) there was never a dull moment.

In 1958 there were 153 white legislators altogether. Of these, 98 were members of the government in power, elected and representing the Nationalist Party; 53 were the opposition, the English-speaking United Party; and two were "white African" representatives, Margaret Ballinger and William Stanford, the voice of the 24 million blacks against the 151 who were the voice of the 3½ million whites. Today even the two white representatives for blacks have been eliminated.

Both as a student and a teacher I had attended scores of meetings which were mostly ordered and disciplined. We attended Parliament as spectators only when they were going to discuss the "native problem." What I was going to see and hear in the House of Assembly—the highest law-making body in the land, supposedly composed of the best legal brains—was going to come as quite a shock to me. Each time a member of the minority opposition stood to put in one good word about how blacks should be treated, he or she would be shouted down with "Sit down, *kaffir-boetie* [nigger-lovers]. Don't speak that language [English] here. This is South Africa."

One time in 1958 we attended a debate on the removal of Africans from the Western Cape before this was enacted into law. One of the greatest proponents of sending Africans into the bantustans was John Vorster, who later became the minister of justice, the prime minister, and finally president of the Republic of South Africa. Then, he was just a back-bencher from some small veld town in the Transvaal, but even in those days one could see in him the excellent potential for a rabid, racist firebrand. On this particular day, before he spoke on the bill to remove Africans from South Africa, he saw us in the spectator section (it was very rare that Africans ever came anywhere near Parliament, which they called their slaughterhouse) and sent a page to inquire if we could understand Afrikaans. When we replied that we could not, he decided to deliver his address to Parliament in English for "our convenience." I was later informed he had never before stooped so low as to address the House in a "foreign language," as if Afrikaans—a bastardized version of Dutch—was not foreign to South Africa.

In his proposal that Africans must be removed from the region around Cape Town, he delivered a horrendous, vitriolic diatribe on Africans. He said only those Africans who were badly needed for manual labor, which was too low even for coloreds, should be allowed to remain. After all, the Western Cape was the natural home of the colored people who were distantly related to whites. His eyes were sick and tired of seeing these black skins in the beautiful Cape of Good Hope Province which God had decreed for the white man and their next of kin only.*

It was high time, he went on, that the Bantu were shipped back to Central Africa around the Equator where the weather was just right for their skins. Blacks were generally uneasy in the company of the white man; that is why manual labor out in the farms and mines was the ideal thing for them. Then, pointing at us as we sat in the gallery upstairs, he said, "Look how uneasy those poor misguided and miseducated creatures up there are. They can hardly look at us, let alone understand what this whole debate is about." When one of my friends, Wandile Kuse, burst into laughter at this monstrous statement, one of the guides escorted him out and we did not see him for the rest of the day. When I met him the following day, he told me that he was warned never to set foot in Parliament again as he was henceforth banned from listening to the "wise and learned" words of the lawmakers—he was "being unappreciative and not understanding" of the whole process.

Vorster continued his harangue. When he said that the opposition members, under their leader de Villiers Graaf, "are going to oppose this bill," one of the government members, I think it was a cabinet minister, interrupted, "No, call him *Sir* de Villiers Graaf, his British title, to show how un-South African he is." The Afrikaner members of Parliament took themselves and their policies very seriously and did their best to ridicule anything British.

This, then, was the level of discussion both in the House of Assembly and in the Senate when it came to discussing matters affecting blacks. To describe the South African Parliament as a

---

*The Afrikaners (European settlers of Dutch descent) considered themselves to be very religious people and quoted from the Bible to prove that black people were meant to be inferior and remain inferior. The Dutch Reformed Churches, three distinct but closely allied churches in South Africa, believe strongly in apartheid. Religious authority is united with political power, as almost all Afrikaners are of the Dutch Reformed Church and make up over 50 percent of the white population.

get-together of conspirators against the African people is really to put it mildly. They are sent to Parliament by their kith and kin to leglislate the best they know how in order to keep the African in perpetual, permanent servility. What is more, they are are paid for it from the blood and sweat shed by the very Africans they would destroy. South Africa's political madness inflicts the same inhumane treatment on the majority of its people as the most repressive fascist states the world has ever known, yet it wants to present to the world the image of a government democratically operated with Parliament and all the fixed machinery in place.

The Founding Conference
of the Pan-Africanist Congress of Azania

In April 1959 I took a couple of days off from my legal work and attended the inaugural conference of the Pan-Africanist Congress of Azania. To this point, the African National Congress was one of the major organizations to articulate the freedom cause for the African people. The ANC had been formed in 1912 more as a protest and reform movement than as a militant forum for revolutionary change. Also there was the Non-European Unity Movement, a federal body espousing the unity of all the oppressed—black, colored and Indian—against South Africa's racist policies. These groups, comprising the Non-European Unity Movement, had a far-left philosophy and an extremely progressive and intellectual following, but they did not have roots within the masses of the people; their members came mainly from the intelligentsia. My group, the CATA, was affiliated with NEUM, as was our colored counterpart, the TLSA.

Annual conferences of the African National Congress were large and representative, but the leadership had always been moderate and patient, hoping that whites would "come around" to an understanding of the needs of Africans. Impatient younger members became frustrated and desired sweeping changes in goals and methods. A resolution of the ANC's annual conference in Kimberly in December 1943 urged the establishment of a Congress Youth League. A core of organizers coalesced in 1944, and the Youth League was formally launched at

151

a meeting on Easter Sunday, 1944, in Johannesburg. The Youth Leaguers were considered rebels and militants working against the conservatism of the older Congress leaders. Under heavy Youth League pressure at the 1949 ANC national conference at Bloemfontein, a "Programme of Action" was adopted which advocated the use of boycotts, strikes, non-cooperation and other forms of civil disobedience. However, throughout the fifties the ANC was still without a clear-cut ideology or plan of action, with some of the leadership lapsing into inactivity rather than accepting the agressive new spirit; others continued with liberal, cautious reformism, while some formed a distinct communist faction.

The Youth League members had just about had enough of delaying tactics. Therefore, a group of young men and women within the ANC formed themselves into an Africanist group and pursued a policy of "Africa for Africans." This group, in the spirit of getting the wagon of freedom moving, called the first convention of the Pan-Africanist Congress. It met at the Orlando Community Hall, Johannesburg, on April 6, 1959—the 307th year to the day that the first Dutch settlers landed on the Cape of Good Hope. The ANC had reached the lowest doldrums of inactivity. It had become purely reformist, with some "liberal" and "red" whites joining to give it proper reformist direction. This was an intolerable state of affairs to the Africanist group which had grown to thousands within the ANC. The PAC, thus, was founded as an independent group with an ideology of its own, separate from the ANC.

The inaugural convention of the Pan-Africanist Congress of Azania was opened by Mangaliso Robert Sobukwe, whom I had known while he was at Fort Hare and I at Lovedale. I attended this historic convention as an observer with the hope of becoming more politically alive and active myself, while at the same time conferring with former college mates about the burning issues of our time. This convention proved to be just what I needed—a political revival session and much more.

In launching the PAC, Sobukwe gave an analytic treatise of what had been, what was then, and what was going to be a South Africa of, by and for the people. He stated with clarity, determination and purpose: "In South Africa we recognize the existence of national groups which are the result of geographical origin within a certain area as well as a shared historical experience of these groups. The Europeans are a foreign minority group which has exclusive control of political, economic, social and military power. It is the dominant group. It is the exploiting group, responsible for the pernicious doctrine of white supremacy which has resulted in the humiliation and degradation of the indigenous African people. It is this group which has dispossessed the African people of their land and with arrogant conceit has set itself up as the 'guardians,' the 'trustees' of the Africans. It is this group which conceives of the African people as a child nation, composed of boys and girls ranging in age from 120 years to one day. It is this group which after 300 years can still state, with brazen effrontery, that the Native, the Bantu, the Kaffir is still backward and savage, et cetera. But they still want to remain 'guardians,' 'trustees,' and what have you, of the African people. It is from this group that the most rabid race baiters and agitators come. It is members of this group who, whenever they meet in their Parliament, say things which agitate the hearts of millions of peace-loving Africans. This is the group which turns out thousands of experts on that new South African science—the Native mind....

"The Africans constitute the indigenous group and form the majority of the population. They are the most ruthlessly exploited and are subjected to humiliation, degradation and insult.... Now it is our contention that true democracy can be established in South Africa, and on the continent as a whole, only when white supremacy has been destroyed. And the illiterate and semi-literate African masses constitute the key and center and content of any struggle for true democracy in South Africa. And the African people can be organized only under the banner of African nationalism in an All-African Organization where they will by themselves formulate policies and programs and decide on the methods of struggle without interference from either so-called left-wing or right-wing groups of the minorities who arrogantly appropriate to themselves the right to plan and think for the Africans.

"We wish to emphasize that the freedom of the African means the freedom of all in South Africa, the European included, because only the African can guarantee the establishment of a genuine democracy in which all men will be citizens of a common state and will live and be governed as individuals and not as distinctive sectional groups."

In regard to the ultimate goals of the PAC, he concluded: "I wish to state that the Africanists do not at all subscribe to the fashionable doctrine of South African exceptionalism. Our contention is that South Africa is an integral part of the indivisible whole that is Africa. She cannot solve her own problem in isolation from and with utter disregard to the rest of the continent.

"Against multi-racialism, we have this objection: that the history of South Africa has fostered group prejudices and antagonisms, and if we have to maintain the same group exclusiveness, parading under the term of multi-racialism, we shall be transporting to the new Africa these very antagonisms and conflicts. Further, multi-racialism is in fact a pandering to European bigotry and arrogance. It is a method of safeguarding white interests irrespective of population figures. In that sense it is a complete negation of democracy. To us the term "multi-racialism implies that there are such basic inseparable differences between the various national groups here that the best course is to keep them permanently distinctive in a kind of democratic apartheid. That to us is racialism multiplied, which probably is what the term truly connotes.

"We aim, politically, at government of the Africans by the Africans for Africans, with everybody who owes his loyalty to Africa and who is prepared to accept the democratic rule of an African majority being regarded as an African. We guarantee no minority rights, because we think in terms of individuals, not groups.

"Economically, we aim at the rapid extension of industrial development in order to alleviate pressure on the land which is what progress means in terms of modern society. We stand committed to a policy guaranteeing the most equitable distribution of wealth.

"Socially, we aim at the full development of the human personality and a ruthless uprooting and outlawing of all forms or manifestations of the racial myth. To sum it up, we stand for an Africanist Socialist Democracy.

"Here is a tree rooted in African soil, nourished with waters from the rivers of Africa. Come and sit under its shade and become, with us, leaves of the same branch and branches of the same tree.

"Then Sons and Daughters of Africa, I declare this inaugural convention of the Africanists open! *IZWE LETHU!* [The land belongs to us]!"[19]

Sobukwe's inaugural address must have been applauded no less than twenty times. You can hear a pin drop when Africans are listening to a speaker, especially about politics. Even unnecessary applause is often considered an interruption. For this group of Africanists to have applauded Sobukwe over twenty times speaks volumes about the seriousness with which his message was received by the crowd. Very few speeches, if any, have ever moved me as much as that one did, and I am not easily moved, either emotionally or intellectually. From the standing ovation at the conclusion of his speech, it was quite clear who the first president of the PAC would be. At the end of the two-day convention, Mangaliso Sobukwe was unanimously elected.

On my return to Cape Town I resumed my usual activities as a law clerk involved in community affairs. Meanwhile the president of the PAC and other officials were touring the country preparing the people for the next stage in the struggle for freedom. In January 1960 Sobukwe came to Cape Town, where he addressed thousands at the Makana Square in Langa. He exhorted the crowd to be ready for the next program of action, to be launched by the PAC within three months. The nature of the action was not specifically spelled out. Details would have to follow from the Central Committee to all regions and branches of the PAC announcing the date and the nature of the campaign. Here again, Sobukwe, who was accompanied by P.K. Leballo, the general secretary of the PAC, was most enthusiastically received.

Early in March the long-awaited clarion call to action was issued. It proclaimed March 21, 1960, as the day when all men would go to the nearest police stations and surrender their passbooks, the most hated of all symbols of oppression. Surrendering these to the police stations where they belonged was just one way—but the beginning of many—in which we were going to strike at oppression. The president's statement to us said, "This is not a game. We are not gambling. We are taking our first step in the march to African independence and the United States of Africa. And we are not leading corpses to the new Africa: we are leading the vital, breathing and dynamic youth of our land. We are leading that youth, *not to death, but to life abundant.* Let us get that clear. . . .

"The principal aim of our Campaign is to get ourselves arrested, get our women remaining at home. This means that nobody will be going to work. Industry will come to a standstill and the government will be forced to accept our terms. And once we score that victory, there will be nothing else we will not be able to tackle. But we must know quite clearly, *now,* that our struggle is an unfolding one, one campaign leading on to another in a *never-ending stream*—until independence is won.

"This is not a game. The white rulers are going to be extremely ruthless. But we must meet their hysterical brutality with calm, iron determination. We are fighting for the noblest cause on earth, the liberation of mankind. They are fighting to entrench an outworn, anachronistic, vile system of oppression. We represent progress. They represent decadence. We represent the fresh fragrance of flowers in bloom; they represent the rancid smell of decaying vegetation. We have the whole Continent on our side. We have history on our side. *We will win!*

"The Government will be ruthless. They will probably try to cut us off from one another, censor the press, use their propaganda machinery to malign the leaders, mislead the people and spread falsehoods about the Campaign. Let nobody depend on either the press or radio. I, myself, Mangaliso Sobukwe, or one of the PAC leaders, acting on my behalf, will call off the struggle, after our demands have been fully met.

"Forward, then, to independence now, tomorrow the United States of Africa!"[20]

The Sharpeville-Langa Massacres of 1960

For over twenty years the United Nations has observed the International Day of Solidarity with the Struggle of the Oppressed in South Africa on March 21. The Sharpeville-Langa Massacres occurred in 1960 on this historic day. I was in Langa, a suburb of Cape Town, on that day that shook the international world as no other event in South Africa had ever done before.

I left work and arrived at the Langa train station at about 6:30 p.m. When I got off the train I was wearing a Rex True-Form three-piece suit and a snow-white shirt, having appeared in court earlier that day. A few minutes before my arrival, thousands of Africans had assembled in the nearby men's flats, ready to march to the nearby police station to surrender their passes. I was on my way to join the protest myself, carrying a briefcase which contained my legal pad, as I had to see some clients in the township later that evening in preparation for a criminal case the following morning in Cape Town's Court B.

I was hardly fifty yards from the station when hundreds of Africans came running, falling on one another and moving towards me shouting, "Run back! They are shooting us!" Shots were ringing from every side. I did not stop to think but joined the crowd of those fleeing—almost an automatic reflex in South Africa. If you're black, your choice is either to move or die. Nobody could keep count of the bodies falling all around. We all just ran for dear life. Police, black and white, had been given the order to "Shoot to kill where you see black." I arrived at my friend Qumbu's house without being shot, though I was bleeding and bruised from having fallen down several times. My suit was torn from jumping over and through fences, and I had lost my briefcase.

What caused this confrontation between police and black South Africans? Two weeks prior to the March 21 resistance marches and subsequent massacres, Sobukwe had been in Langa and I had met with him to renew our academic and political ties. During the planning for the peaceful protests, I had served as legal advisor to the organizers. The passbook protests were planned for all the major cities of South Africa. In Johannesburg Sobukwe himself, a Methodist-reared university instructor, led a group of protestors to the Orlando police station and was arrested. When he was released nine years later, he was wracked with cancer and died soon after, in 1978.

The biggest rallies were held in Sharpeville, a black township about twenty-eight miles from Johannesburg where twenty thousand Africans turned out; and in Langa, five miles from

Cape Town, where an almost equally large number answered the call. Many other thousands protested and rallied in townships like Evaton and Van Der Byl Park in the Vaal region and in the cities of East London, Port Elizabeth, Durban, Bloemfontein and Pretoria. Men, women and children of all ages came together to descend upon local police stations—without arms, without violence—to reject the hated passbook. Mothers with babies on their backs, the frail elderly, the crippled and ill, all peacefully came out to return those badges of slavery to the police stations, enforcers of apartheid. The march was like a funeral dirge, with occasional low sounds of *"Sifuna izwe lethu* [We want our land]" and solemn singing of *"Sikhalela izwe lethu, elathathwa ngabamhlophe* [We cry for our land, which was taken by the whites]."

Protests were held in the morning except in Langa, an extension of Cape Town, where they were scheduled for late afternoon to allow for majority black participation. Many blacks were expected to converge from surrounding black townships like Nyanga, Retreat, Simonstown and Kensington, and from scattered "white areas" like Athlone, Wynberg, District 6 and Muizenberg. And indeed they came, thousands of men and women determined to peacefully protest against the oppressive apartheid in general and against the pass laws in particular. In every area the people were suppressed by the threat of guns in the hands of white authorities. From then to the present, the white South African government has placed faith in guns, terror and formidable military superiority to settle basic human problems.

In spite of this unfolding of history, my life returned to its regular patterns of existence the next day. I rushed home to Salt River, quickly changed clothes and went to meet the clients I had failed to meet the night before. I was standing outside B Court in Caledon Square with my two clients when about half a dozen young, white policemen ordered everybody either to go inside the court or go home immediately. When I told them my case was to be called next in B Court and that I was for the defense, they replied, "No kaffirs allowed outside courtrooms."

I asked, "Since when would a lawyer not be allowed to consult with clients?"

They replied, "Since always," and started beating us heavily with their batons. You should have seen me run up Darling Street to our offices on St. Georges Street!

By the way, the briefcase that I had dropped when I was running in Langa the night before has not been found to this day. Only the police could have picked it up; no one else had the time while running at maximum speed. People lost shoes and left coats, shirts and dresses hanging on fences. Even the papers on which I had been taking notes outside B Court I let fly into the street when I ran from Caledon Square.

A few days after the Sharpeville-Langa Massacre, it become known that hundreds had been imprisoned in the Roeland Street Jail, in the heart of Cape Town. I was "privileged" to visit a few inmates since I was an articled clerk. There I saw hundreds packed into cells with hardly the space to move. Some had to stand to take their meals of unbuttered bread and hot water. I could see my old friend, advocate Harry Bloom, in the white-segregated part of the prison. He was one of many lawyers noted for advancing the African cause and had been detained under the emergency laws which allowed no charge be given for arrest. The "ninety-day" law of detention or jail without charges dates from March 1960 and is still in existence today.

Even after March 21, hundreds of people who wished to make their contribution towards removing the chains binding blacks in South Africa surrendered or destroyed their passes. Prominent among these was the late Chief Albert Luthuli, president of the African National Congress and the 1961 Nobel Peace Prize winner. This noted pacifist burned his passbook in Johannesburg in full view of the press.

In Cape Town the culminating point of protest was the march of around 100,000 men and women whose aim was to storm the Parliament. The Parliament building was surrounded by white soldiers armed to the teeth and ready to kill any black who ventured near the building. While the crown was held at bay outside the tall, pointed wrought-iron fence surrounding the Parliament grounds, several of the more mature and seemingly less severe police chiefs, accompanied by Patrick Duncan, a long time proponent of black rights and head of the Liberal Party, stepped forward and invited the leaders of the march, headed by Philip Kgosana, to meet inside the building. The protest leaders were told they could voice the complaints of the people to the Minister of Justice. The leaders never reappeared before the crowd. Inside they were arrested forthwith and were held without bail for over a year.

I was in the crowd myself. We were told the conference with the leaders would take a long time. So with dusk coming on and miles to walk for many before arriving home, the crowd dispersed. The black Africans were to learn from experiences like this that the white man's promises and actions were without honor. Experience is the best teacher, but the most expensive. That very evening the racist regime declared a state of emergency thoughout the country and hurriedly passed legislation banning the PAC and the ANC. Students at the University of Natal assembled on campus, and in place of the South African flag they hoisted banners reading "Hitler 1939, Verwoerd 1960."*

These liberation attempts were followed by a temporary reprive of thirty days from carrying passes, ordered by the minister of justice, John Balthaazar Vorster. Vorster later said in Parliament that Sobukwe, the leader of the movement, would be kept in jail "till this side of eternity" after serving his original three-year term for protesting passes, a statement worthy of his name. (Balthaazar is a Biblical right-hand man of Satan.) Vorster later became prime minister and then president of South Africa. He was forced out of office in 1979 in a Watergate-style scandal when it was revealed he had been involved in the illegal spending of millions of dollars to buy an American newspaper network to propagate the "good" of apartheid. After decades of advocating the sinful apartheid, he fell ignominiously.

---

*A.F. Verwoerd, an ardent champion of the Afrikaner Nationalist Part, dominated South African politics for almost two decades. He stated in 1961, "I see it as a party which stands for the preservation of the white man, of white government in South Africa." He was an architect of the Bantu Education Act and was instrumental in developing the "homelands" policy. He held several positions in party and government, among them minister of native affairs in 1950 and prime minister from 1958 to 1966, when he was assassinated.

It was finally reported to the world that the South African government had met peaceful demonstrators on March 21, 1960, with Sabre jets and Harvard Trainers zooming within one hundred feet of the ground, and with Saracen armored cars in the streets. Sixty-nine Africans were killed within five minutes by police fire in Sharpeville. Countless others who were wounded or massacred in other ways were never reported. An independent commission was set up in April by a liberal organization called the Race Relations Committee to collect and collate facts from individuals who had been on the scene. The committee was headed by advocate Donald Molteno of the Supreme Court. Many African residents volunteered to appear before the committee, and two African policemen who had resigned from the force since the massacre volunteered as well.

I attended the session of the Molteno Commission when these two policemen testified. Up till this day, twenty-two years later, my body shivers when I remember what one black policeman reported: "We black policemen were ordered to dig a mass grave in the bushes beyond the men's flats at about midnight. Those protesters who had been critically wounded that night were rushed to the Langa Hospital. But when all the beds were used up, we were ordered to take the almost hopeless cases to the police "mortuary." After we had completed the mass grave, we were told to throw the helpless and hopeless cases in there in their clothes, boots and all. I cannot forget the last words of [a man] who knew me. He said, 'Oh son, do you not see I am still alive? Why bury me alive? What will your ancestors say?' That is why I handed in my police uniform the following day. I was ordered never to divulge this information. I do not want my name ever to appear in your report lest I, too, be shot or jailed for life. . . ."

The Molteno Commission Report has never been published, either in South Africa or abroad. Much information has been smuggled out of the country about the atrocities and the genocide, but never the Molteno Report. I do not know why. Unfortunately, Donald Molteno, who was a friend of mine, is himself dead now, of old age.

Youths Charged With Public Violence and Arson

While the police were murdering on the evening of March 21, some administration buildings, especially those that processed passes, were set on fire and burned down. Several other buildings, especially those that accomodated government officials, were also either stoned or burned down. Damage was estimated in the thousands of dollars. What seemed unclear was who could have had the time to commit all these "crimes," since almost all those on the streets were on the run from police bullets. Those who were not on the run were definitely inside their houses.

About fifty youths, almost all teenagers, were arrested that night or the following morning and charged with the crimes of public violence and arson. Our law firm was retained to defend the accused. The state could not have had a very good case, especially in obtaining witnesses to the act of arson—who could have been standing as an onlooker? It was really no surprise, then, when after about a month's trial all the accused persons in this case were acquitted.

Two of us at my firm handled the defense: a white senior member of our firm, a very good lawyer, and myself. I did most of the interviewing and took statements inside the jail and in the cellars of the courthouse at Caledon Square, where the case was being heard. The parents and relatives of my clients gave me some ointments which looked like petroleum jelly to give to each client for use when he appeared in court. The accused would smear part of his face with this medicine, which was then supposed to affect the outcome of the case. I was also to pass on instructions as to their use. I knew it would boost morale, and this is what any lawyer wishes for his client. Pragmatism often has to supersede rationality.

When all the defendants in that case were acquitted, the question of whether or not witchcraft played any role at all became moot. The case was in good legal hands, and the defense lawyer's arguments had succeeded by legal validity. But as my Xhosa traditional background has met Western thought and modern practices. I have come to believe that perhaps witchcraft and divination are really not too different from some psychiatric methods.

Leaving South Africa

One weekend in December of that year a group of my political friends from the Transvaal and I decided to camp on Cape Point and review the events of the year as a Christmas festival. It was a beautiful summer weekend, with temperatures reaching the nineties. This is one of the most enjoyable seasons of the Cape, as the breeze from both oceans allows for no humidity and sultriness. Hundreds of comrades and freedom fighters had been jailed for long terms since the March uprisings in Sharpville and Langa. Some of us were being sought by the police. We discussed the state of the nation, what we as Africans could do to change the racist system, and the fate of most of our leaders past and present who were jailed for militating against colonialism, imperialism and oppression.

Six miles to our east, in the Atlantic Ocean, lies Robben Island, where 95 percent of the people considered most dangerous to the racist regime are held. Robben Island had been a leper colony for the early Dutch settlers in the sixteenth century. People who had to be weaned from society, such as the mentally insane, spent their last days on the island.* Here Mangaliso Sobukwe served three years of his nine-year sentence. Other prominent leaders of the African people still languish on Robben Island, including Nelson Mandela and Walter Sisulu, who were sentenced to life imprisonment for their roles in the leadership of the African National Congress.

---

*In his book *Robben Island,* Indres Naidoo writes: "...[The prisons had] no running water or sewage in the cells. It was filthy, and had the atmosphere of a Gestapo camp with barbed wire everywhere and armed wardens on posts, just as we had seen in films about the Nazis." After a ten- to twelve-hour day working at the quarries on the island, the author sums it up: "Our arms ached; our hands were blistered. Our backs were sore. Our necks were stiff. Our eyes stung. Our skins prickled. Still we kept on hammering and hammering without stop, all day, under the boiling sun."

Once, Naidoo recalls, when he was caught smoking, he was so brutally caned as a punishment that he collapsed. For three weeks he could hardly sit on his backside, and he states, "To this day I still sleep on my stomach." Prisoners sick with flu, asthma, fits or eye trouble were all given castor oil. The author recalls several cases of patients sent to hospitals on the mainland who died immediately upon arrival. Prison officials are suspected of having murdered black prisoners without being censured or investigated by higher authorities.

Another is Zephania Mothupeng, a founder and leader of the Pan-Africanist Congress of Azania, who was sentenced to thirty years in 1979 at the age of sixty-five for his role in leading the Soweto Uprising of 1976. Under no circumstances does South African law allow for probation or remission of sentence for so-called political prisoners, yet murderers, rapists and thieves are entitled to a one-third period of remission for their crimes.

We also talked about Nxele Makana, the first-ever "political" prisoner on Robben Island in the mid-nineteenth century. He came from the Eastern Cape around Grahamstown, close to the Indian Ocean. He was an accredited leader of the rural farmers, esteemed by chiefs and peasants equally. He traveled to many areas and presided over meetings discussing the "white problem." Whites had not only stolen cattle but were still penetrating further inland grabbing more land from the indigenous Africans. Instead of killing the whites outright, he proposed that they be driven back to where they began. The whites had come by way of the sea, so he campaigned throughout the length and breadth of the Eastern Cape that they be driven back to the sea. From there they would find their way home. The Africans were not interested in escorting them to their land—after all, Africans had enough land of their own which they intended to keep and protect without spilling the white man's blood on it.

It was during this worthwhile campaign that the British, who had long since joined the Dutch in the rape of the land, seized Nxele Makana and took him as prisoner to Robben Island. There he was held in solitary confinement away from the lepers and only allowed out of his cell for brief periods of time to exercise. Each time he was out of his cell he could clearly see the mainland Cape Town city; at night its lights seemed to beckon him, flashing the message from his people: "Come back home. We need your leadership." I can better imagine than describe what must have been going on in this patriot's mind night and day when he could only communicate with his captors and the sea waves, yet his people were just a few miles inland. During one of these excruciating moments he decided to plunge into the sea and swim towards Table Bay and freedom. The story has it that he drowned; whether or not this is true or he was murdered on the island is of no particular substance to us now. We lost one of our pioneer freedom fighters in very suspicious circumstances.

Up to the time of this writing, over forty-five prisoners awaiting trial have been murdered in South African prisons through "self-hangings" or "jumping accidents." We have heard these stories before. They have become the stock-in-trade of the South African racist regime, its way of eliminating its opponents. We need only mention the 1977 murder of Steve Biko, who came from the same area as Makana. He was arrested by police less than ten miles from Makana's former home.

As we sat up there on the Cape Point in the dusk of that December evening, smoking and sipping beer, we could see the fluorescent and electric lights on Robben Island beckoning to us, saying, "Come along, we are waiting for those who would destroy our granite regime. Come, your turn is next on Robben Island." We were so near, yet so far. That weekend my friends and I discussed until dawn the advisability of continuing the fight for freedom at home and thus becoming candidates for inmateship on Robben Island or any of the other thousands of prisons in South Africa whose mouths gape open, ready to swallow anyone who dares challenge white supremacy. Strong views were advanced that the battle was at home. Escaping either by sea to Europe or even up north within Africa would be a sell-out. We should die or drown in our beloved South Africa as Makana had done.

Some asked, what use can we be if we allow ourselves to rot in South African jails? Surely the masses of our people needed what little leadership we could give. If we were to go up north, to the African countries that were already liberated, we could mobilize whatever assistance the brothers and sisters could give there and return home to fight the enemy. We were about equally divided on this issue.

Late Sunday afternoon we packed our camping materials and headed for the city, where my friends from the Transvaal would entrain for their homes. I have not seen them since, but I have heard about and from some of them. As for myself, I headed for the Transkei a few days later to say goodbye to my mother and the country where I was born and which had nurtured me. I was saying goodbye, but only for a while. Someday I will be back in a free Azania.

The decision to leave South Africa for some unknown destination to prepare myself for the overthrow of the racist regime was certainly one of the most agonizing and difficult ones I hope ever to make. My roots are in South Africa: my home, my people and above all my land, I am South Africa and South Africa is me. It can be no other way. Nothing short of complete equality among all South African people will ever be satisfactory. That is why many of us are determined to see a liberated South Africa by any means possible, even if death is necessary. After all, a few must die in a revolution so that hundreds and thousands of others may live to enjoy freedom. Freedom, just like life, cannot be had in degrees: you are either free or not free, alive or dead.

I left South Africa because I could not reconcile myself with the status quo. I also thought I could be more useful outside of jail rather than in a South African jail as long as I was going to be organizing vehemently against the system wherever I was and at any time.

My First Exit

When ultimately I left Cape Town in January 1961, it was because I had very little choice. I had been tipped off one Tuesday afternoon when I was in court that the Special Branch Police had just obtained a warrant for my arrest that day and would probably be checking on me that very night. I had long suspected this was coming. I would have to leave sooner than I had anticipated. That night I did not go home; a friend of mine picked up those items of mine that were essential for my departure.

The following day a friend drove me out of Cape Town to catch a train at Bellville station. This was about six miles away, where I would not be as readily recognized as in the downtown station. As we drove along, I looked through the window and said goodbye to that "fairest" Cape of them all. Two lines from the poetry of Walter de LaMare came to mind as we drove:

> *Look thy last on all things lovely*
> *Every hour.*

Why was I leaving at all? In my land of birth blacks were still burning in the flames of injustice, were still crippled by the manacles of apartheid, were still held in poverty within the vast ocean of material prosperity. But I could no longer endure the human degradation which I could not cure, at least from within South Africa. I was in search of tools to procure for myself and my compatriots the inalienable rights of life, liberty and the pursuit of happiness, to prepare more intensively in many ways for the coming revolution. I was not quitting the struggle. I was not then, nor am I now, nor shall I ever be, a quitter when it comes to fighting to repossess my land. The sunlit path of racial justice has to be found to replace the dark and desolate valley of apartheid. I was hoping to join that band of brothers and sisters who had gone abroad sworn to the idea that South Africa must be freed by whatever means possible during our lifetime. No doubt the path would be full of trials and tribulations—so were many things that were for the good of humanity—but there surely would be glimpses of light at the end of the tunnel.

I was saying goodbye to the curvaceous peaks of Cape Point; I was leaving the beautiful ridges of Simonstown on the Atlantic Ocean. How difficult it is to part with what is closest to your heart, especially the creations of nature itself! Life would continue wherever I was until that day of reckoning came when South Africa would be as it should be: free for all its peoples.

I boarded the train at the Bellville station and proceeded north as far as Mafeking, which is northwest of the Cape and the last city on the border before entering the then-Bechuanaland. There was not much screening at the border in those days. South Africans visiting Botswana simply had to say they were visiting friends for a day or two. All they had to do was show their passes and that was enough. Botswana citizens used to shop in Mafeking; all they had to do was declare this to get into South Africa, so crossing the South African border into Botswana was certainly quite simple this first time. I was out of South Africa. Little did I realize this would be a long exile into agony.

8

Botswana, Temporary Home for an Exile

My final destination in Botswana was to Moeng College, one of two high schools in the country. Two of my friends from Fort Hare taught there, and I hoped to get the feel of the land from them. They had been in Botswana for over two years.

The nearest railway station to Moeng was Palapye; from the station there was only one means of transportation to the college about twenty miles away: the school truck, which came to the railway station on Wednesdays and Saturdays. Fortunately, I arrived on a Saturday morning and had to wait for only three hours before the truck arrived with some teachers and students on a shopping spree. This was the nearest shopping center to the school, with three different shops, a bar and a police station. All together, there were no more than ten buildings, all single-story, in the whole village of Palapye. I was told that I could wait for my teacher friends at the bar as soon as it opened at 9:00 a.m.—my friends were sure to come there since it was the only bar servicing a forty-mile radius. I was to find out that there were actually more cattle than people in Botswana, millions of cattle compared to about half a million people. This certainly reinforced the statements in the geography books that Botswana was pastoral land lying mainly in the Kalihari Desert!

While I was at the station, smoking a cigarette and waiting for everything to open, I saw two boys chasing two dogs. The dogs were dragging smelly pieces of meat which looked like legs from a dead beast. The boys retrieved the meat from the dogs and proceeded to make a fire over which they roasted and ate some of the meat. The rest of the carcass, which they also retrieved from the dogs, they carried home. I asked some of the people at the station if this was a common occurence. I was told that there was much starvation, and those who did not have their own animals or were too lazy to go hunting actually lived like that. Poverty and starvation were abundant in South Africa, yet I had never competed with dogs for something to eat; we were discouraged from eating anything that we found lying around dead when we did not know how it had died. I felt on this very first day like someone in a strange land with altogether different customs. To compound everything I could speak little or no Tswana, the language of the land, and most of the folks I had met so far did not or could not speak English. As I look back at those first months in Botswana, I realize most of my thoughts were influenced by homesickness, ethnocentrism and culture shock.

At 9:00 I went into the Palapye bar and ordered a drink. This was the first time in my entire life I had had a drink in a bar side by side with a few white people. There were no bars at all for Africans in South Africa, not even segregated ones. We could buy what was then called "European" liquor with a special permit, but it could not be consumed on the premises; we had to take it home. Segregated bars and liquor stores were not opened in South Africa until 1962. So on that Saturday morning in Palapye I had already acquired some "freedom." When my friends from Moeng College finally joined me at about noon at the bar, we reminisced about our college days and they briefed me without much detail about Botswana and how to go about asking for temporary political asylum. Late in the afternoon we drove to the college, where I was to remain for a few days until I had been granted asylum by the district commissioner.

It took about two hours to drive the twenty miles to Moeng. The weather was described to me as quite normal, meaning there usually was no rainfall. The "roads" were such that trucks and lorries had to travel at a snail's pace. Tires rolling on the roadbed of rocks and stones were likely to be punctured at any time. Often the road ended and the few vehicles continued

170

on through the brushwood. We went up and down hill until we finally reached Moeng, which lies on a beautiful, flat piece of land. I was surprised: Moeng was very modern-looking after the terrain we had just gone through. There was running water and even windmill-generated electricity. I noticed some teachers even had oil-operated refrigerators. When I inquired about the possibility of a teaching job right there at Moeng, I was told that unfortunately they were fully staffed.

I stayed at Moeng for a week while I was arranging an interview with the district commissioner of the Bamangwato area. Moeng was in the Bamangwato jurisdictional district and the commissioner's office was at Serowe, about fifty miles away, where the nearest hospital for the school was located. I spent my days either reading or just sitting in on some classes taught by my friends. Though I very much liked taking walks, I did not feel much like doing so because the place was infested with what I considered to be my worst non-human enemies: reptiles. I had even seen a few crawling right in the school yard, and I was unpleasantly surprised to see the Tswana boys actually catching some snakes alive by the head. It seemed that Botswana had more snakes than people as well.

After a week I was granted political asylum by the district commissioner, Mr. Robinson, and given a place to live with about six other South African exiles in Serowe. The International Defense and Aid Fund, a humanitarian organization with headquarters in London, provided food, shelter and clothing assistance to southern African refugees wherever they were. From them we received meals and occasional reading material. There were no jobs we could look for in Botswana. There wasn't any industry or much farming; about 80 percent of Botswana's population worked in South Africa. The Ngwato* people around

---

*Bamangwato is the plural form and refers to the Ngwato people. The Africans in Botswana are Batswana of southern Sotho stock and are related to the people of Lesotho. Tswana is the most common African tongue, although the official language is English. The Batswana are composed of eight main groupings: Bamangwato, Bakwena, Batawana, Bangwaketse, Bakgatla, Bamalete, Barolong and Batlokwa.

171

Serowe were the kindest I ever came across in Botswana. They really cared for strangers, whom the called *Baeng!* When you buy beer among the Bamangwato, the tradition is that the saleswoman lets you taste about a cupful to see if it meets with your approval. If you don't like the taste, you are allowed to pass on to the next house, which may have just the type you like. As South African refugees, we were broke most of the time, so we would start sampling beer, usually about 9:00 a.m. In each house we pretended the beer was not quite what we were looking for, and in this manner we passed from house to house until about noon, when we found that we had had enough beer just through sampling. The Bamangwato people did not mind our continuing for many days to "taste" beer. They had the beer and we needed some. It was often our principal source of energy and nutrition.

Apart from reading two or three day-old papers from South Africa and reading whatever books I could lay my hands on, the days were dull and slow-moving. Botswana was one of the least industrialized countries of Africa in 1961. Even dry cleaning had to be sent either to Mafeking, South Africa, or Bulawayo, Rhodesia. The ten months from February to November seemed like ten years.

The PAC was busy putting up offices abroad so as to be able to monitor the freedom fighters as they came out of South Africa. People were going to be assigned to duties according to their abilities and needs. Some would go straight to military training, others to schools of one kind or another, others to administrative duties. Since I was not yet ready for military training and did not really need further education compared to the others, I was on the waiting list and could take a job where any of my skills could be utilized. This would not only help me but would also help the party as I would give some of my salary for the upkeep of the organization.

My Second Escape

When I escaped from South Africa I thought that black South Africans would gain enough support, both internally and internationally, that my return to the country of my birth would be a magnificent re-entry into a free world, or at least a commitment to support a revolution. Never had I envisioned being brought back in handcuffs by husky Afrikaner policemen. I never even dreamed a second escape from South Africa would be necessary.

There were only two high schools, Moeng and St. Josephs, one teacher training school (in Lobatsi) and about five secondary schools in the whole country of Botswana. All were fully staffed with about 80 percent black South Africans, 10 percent British and 10 percent Botswana personnel. The British had ruled Botswana for about seventy-six years as a British protectorate. Recent figures show how much the British had protected the Botswana people from being educated; in the seventeen years since its independence from Britain, Botswana has developed about ten times as many high schools plus a university, with 50 percent of its teaching staff drawn from local inhabitants.

I was now living in Serowe at the home of a South African woman named Tsidi Ntjana from East London, who taught at the Sekgoma Higher Primary School. We had met around March and soon started to date. It was lovely to have someone of the opposite sex to fill the social vacuum, and my association with her saved me from living in the South African refugee camp, where the poverty was horrible. We even took walks around Serowe, which did not have as many snakes as the area around Moeng.

Every Christmas vacation Tsidi returned home to South Africa. By the time the schools closed for Christmas in Botswana, I had made arrangements to get to the next country up north, Southern Rhodesia (now Zimbabwe),* in search of a way of earning a living, preferably by teaching. I had contacted my former colleagues and other friends from Rhodesia with whom I had worked in Cape Town, and they were trying to find jobs and accomodations for me in Rhodesia.

As we stood at the railway station at Palapye, Tsidi waiting to board the train to East London and I ready to board one north

---

*Part of the then-Federation of Northern and Southern Rhodesia and Nyasaland, now Zimbabwe, Zambia and Malawi.

to Rhodesia, one of those delicate love scenes known the world over was enacted. My beloved was returning to South Africa, a home I had involuntarily abandoned, while I was heading for an unknown destination to begin a new life in a strange land, among strange people of different minds. I was parting with someone who had meant very much to me during the previous ten months. What man does not depend on the encouragement, joy, companionship and love of a woman in times of happiness and in times of travail! We warmly embraced and kissed each other goodbye, tears streaming from our eyes. We did not know when or where we might meet again. Why could this not go on forever? I asked myself. Why this politicizing? Cannot I just join Tsidi on her return to South Africa and compromise with the powers that be? I could serve my jail sentence for political activities as others had to do. "Anywhere is nowhere, there is only one home," ran through my head.

But forward ever, backward never. I was determined to go back to South Africa only when it was possible to change the oppression there. My consolation was that others had gone abroad before me to prepare themselves and others—through education and military training—for the inevitable, ultimate revolution in South Africa. I was going to join in enlisting the sympathy and subsequent aid of the civilized world. As the train pulled off with Tsidi aboard, I mumbled half-heartedly to myself Cassius' farewell to Brutus:

> *Forever and forever farewell, Tsidi*
> *If we meet again, why, we shall smile indeed,*
> *If not, then this parting was well made.*

Since the Federation of Rhodesia and Nyasaland had excellent diplomatic relations with South Africa, I knew the customs officials would require South African documents in order for me to cross the border. Therefore, I had borrowed a Botswana tax receipt from a friend, all that was needed of Botswana citizens to cross the border into Zimbabwe at Plumtree at that time. As a "citizen" of Botswana, I had no problem crossing the border. While in Botswana as a political refugee, I

174

was under the Queen's protection and could not be extradited to South Africa. Or so I thought.

I alighted at the Bulawayo railway station. Bulawayo is the major city of western Zimbabwe. The inhabitants are mostly the Ndebele people, and their language, Ndebele, is very close to Xhosa. Ndebel, Xhosa, Swazi and Zulu form what is known as the Nguni group of Southern African languages. (The other major group is the Sotho, which consists of Sotho and Tswana.)

At the Bulawayo Railway Station is a plaque which explains how that city earned its name. *Kwa bulawayo* means a place of killing or slaughter. The city is positioned on the original site of the palace of the king of the AmaNdebele, Mzilikazi. When the whites arrived in 1883, they wanted the best of the land of Mzilikazi. It was here, then, that the bloodiest confrontations took place. Scores of men fell on both sides: the blacks from the bullets and cannons of the British, the British from the spears and poisoned arrows of the forces of Mzilikazi. For weeks the valiant Ndebele forces withstood British cannons until the battalion of Lobengula, who would succeed Mzilikazi after his death by old age, surrendered. Until then, the country was known as Zimbabwe, but following the battle, the British quickly renamed it Rhodesia, after Cecil Rhodes. Rhodes left England as a lad of seventeen because he could not be cured of tuberculosis in England. He settled in Kimberley, South Africa, where the weather was excellent, and was cured almost immediately. After completing his schooling at Oxford University, he returned to South Africa, where he is supposed to have discovered the diamond mines of Kimberley. He soon became a multimillionaire. Later he became prime minister of the Cape Province and used part of his fortune to develop the University of Cape Town. His statue stands outside the Houses of Parliament in Cape Town and on the campus of the University, pointing north, ever hoping "to build a railway line from Cape Town to Cairo."

When Rhodesia became independent in 1980, one of the first acts of the people's government was to remove his statue and other such relics of colonialism. Any of his statues still standing in racist South Africa are destined for the same fate. As I write these lines my heart rejoices that the country of Zimbabwe has been repossessed by the people. Rhodesia is gone and forgotten, South Africa is still there. Can it be too long before it becomes Azania, the name which the people already use? If spring is here, can summer be far away?

In Bulawayo I lived in the township of Mpopoma with friends I had known in Cape Town. I had a good time there and stayed for about two weeks, before Christmas 1961. I frequently visited old colleagues in the townships of Mzilikazi, Lobengula and Luveve—beautiful people and places named in honor of valiant leaders. The one and only liberation organization at that time was the National Democratic Party, whose president was Joshua Nkomo. The general secretary, George Silundika, and the publicity secretary, Robert Mugabe, had been my colleagues at Fort Hare in the early fifties; they were all based in the capital of Salisbury (now Harare), where the NDP had its headquarters.

In mid-December the National Democratic Party was banned as a "subversive" organization by the government of Sir Edgar Whitehead. Its Land Rovers, used for national organizing, all office equipment in all cities where it had offices, documents, and other party paraphenalia were confiscated by the government. The NDP's biggest offices were in Harare and Bulawayo. After its banning, the country had no legal people's party opposing the white settler government. This situation was indeed astonishing and hypocritical when one considers that the colonial rulers declared that they were ruling African countries only until the people could govern themselves. Here was an example of African people trying to gain political experience in organizing their own political party on a national level, as they had used democratic processes at the local level, yet this democratic process was denied to them.

About the time of the banning of the NDP, I moved to Harare, where the country's main education department was located. After one or two interviews I was hired as a teacher at the then-Salisbury African Secondary School in Harare Township. I stayed at the home of George T. Silundika. Three or four houses up the road lived Robert Mugabe. By the time I arrived at Harare these two stalwarts were among the former officials of the NDP who were drafting the constitution of a new party, the

Zimbabwe African People's Union. Since schools had not yet
reopened after the holidays, my former colleagues soon co-
opted me and put me to work helping draft the constitution.
Among the leaders of the new ZAPU party were two other Fort
Hare colleagues, Dr. Julius Parirenyatwa and attorney Herbert
Chitepo. We had all belonged to the African National Congress
Youth League, so this was a coincidental and happy reunion.
Almost every day in downtown Harare, where ZAPU had
opened its new offices, I could be seen in the company of either
one or more of these recognized leaders of Zimbabwe whose old
political party had just been banned. Although I was a new face
in town, I became quite conspicuous in the reflected light of
these important men. Since this association identified me
politically, people started wondering who I really was.

When schools opened in January for the beginning of the first
term in the new school year in Zimbabwe, I went to take up my
first teaching post since my dismissal under Bantu Education
six years before then. I was teaching the second class of the day
during my very first day at the Salisbury Secondary School
when the principal came to inform me that two gentlemen from
the justice department were waiting to see me in his office. I immediately left the class and went to see them. They identified
themselves as immigration officials and said they were there to
arrest me and return me to South Africa where I was wanted
for my political crimes. I was told I would have no time even to
return to the classroom to pick up my briefcase. The principal
quickly brought it to me. The immigration officials accompanied
me to their car, where they handcuffed me before taking me to
the police station. At the police station I was formally charged
with having entered the country illegally. The police stated I
was being extradited to South Africa to face whatever charges
they might bring against me; I would be flown back to Johannesburg that afternoon. I pleaded that I be taken to Highfields,
where I lived, in order to collect my belongings. This favor was
refused, and I was told that my belongings would be shipped
after me, that it would not be in the best interest of peace and
order to allow me to enter the township again as I was an illegal
alien. I was then locked up in a separate cell with half a loaf of

bread and a mug of coffee for my lunch to wait to be taken to the airport at 3:00.

When I was applying for a teaching position, I had given all the necessary details about myself, where I was born, and of course, my academic transcripts which had my proper South African name. I suspect that the company I had kept with Mugabe, Silundika and other political figures prompted the authorities to investigate me in depth. Though I knew I had no authorized papers to enter the country, I felt confident that I would not be deported since I had not committed any crime in the English sense of the word. But the order of my deportation was apparently legal, as it had been signed by the prime minister of the Federation of Rhodesia and Nyasaland, Sir Roy Wellensky. Apparently the Federation took a very different view from the British Crown.

I boarded the British Overseas Airways Corporation plane that fateful afternoon at the Salisbury Airport. It was the first airplane trip of my life. I was in handcuffs and accompanied by a British South African policeman. When the plane was about to take off, he removed the handcuffs and left. I sat alone at the back of the plane. I could move up and down the aisle like the rest of the passengers when I wanted to go to the bathroom. There was one black woman on board, a former Miss Makiwane who had married a Zimbabwean and was going to South Africa on a visit to her parents, whom I had known in Umtata. I chatted with her in Xhosa. As I had only a tickey, or three pennies, on my person, I asked her for some money in case I might need it when I got off the plane. Since I had explained my plight to her, she gladly gave me five shillings.

I now contemplated the future during my last few minutes as a free man. I knew very well what was awaiting me on my arrival in South Africa. It was a foregone conclusion that I was going to be charged with having left the country without a legal document. The minimum sentence at that time for this was six months' imprisonment without the option of paying a fine. For any of the other political crimes I was alleged to have committed, I could get up to twenty years' imprisonment. And I thought with dread of Robben Island. As the plane flew over the Limpopo River, which separates Zimbabwe from South Africa, and as the stewardess announced the plane's position, how I wished the plane would crash into the river! I would have nothing much to lose but my life, and I would avoid going to jail. I had read of plane crashes and had sympathized with the victims and their families. This time I would not be around to sympathize; instead, others would have to bear the burden. But the stewardess soon announced, "Fasten your seat belts; we will soon be landing in Jan Smuts Airport in Johannesburg."

Although I had been to Johannesburg several times before this, I had never been anywhere near the airport. The plane landed. I was the last to leave, and a husky Afrikaner policeman and his partner were waiting at the exit door with handcuffs ready to clamp onto my small wrists. I was led to the customs police office, where I sat with my two guardians. They told me we would wait for about half an hour for the chief of the political security police, Colonel Spengler, to arrive and assign me to a jail either in Cape Town or the Transkei. I was to spend the first night at a police station in Johannesburg.

They teased me a lot. "You stupid kaffir, how could you leave this beautiful country without a proper passport?"

I stood up obligingly, with a show of servility, saying, "You're right, boss. I will never make that mistake again. That Rhodesia country is horrible. I am so glad to return home. In fact, I am very thankful to my government for paying my way back. I was just waiting for my first paycheck and I was going to come right back. Food is no good there and I cannot even speak the language of those *Makwerekwere* [a derogatory word referring to all non-South African blacks]."

This dialogue seemed to impress them. I heard them say to each other in the Afrikaans language which they thought I could not understand, "He is a good, small kaffir. He realizes that he was misled by these communist agitators." Then they addressed me again. "So you don't like them Rhodesian boys who come here to work in the mines?"

I replied, "Not at all. Actually, you should send them back to their stupid country. They come here to take our jobs."

They rallied back, "You are right, John, but then you boys don't want to work in the kitchens, gardens or mines. Rhodesian boys are good workers for us. They take anything we give them."

So went the conversation for about fifteen minutes. When I was convinced they were satisfied that I was one of the good boys and that I was very repentant, I asked them for a favor: to be allowed to go to the bathroom, which was about ten yards away. Blacks did not use inside bathrooms; they had to use outhouses. My two guardians readily agreed. One of them accompanied me halfway. Because of the segregated aspect of the bathrooms and because I had told him I was going to empty my bowels, he simply loosened the handcuffs from one hand and let me go alone. He warned though, "Make quick and come back."

"Yes, my boss, I'll make quick."

As I was about to enter the bathroom, I looked back and saw that he was returning to the customs police office. It was about 5:00 p.m. Scores of airport workers were going home, heading to the nearest railway station, Isando. The people were rushing, even running to the station. I pushed the handcuffs up my right sleeve, put my right hand in my trouser pocket and followed the crowd rushing to the railway station. I jumped onto the train like everybody else and was soon on my way to downtown Park Station in Johannesburg. In Johannesburg you pay your fare inside the train, and that's exactly what I did, with the half crown Miss Makiwane had given me. Again I was on a temporary sojourn of freedom; how long this would last, only time would tell.

As soon as I got off the train at Park Station, I rushed to the men's room. As I went in the door I bumped into a former Fort Hare colleague, Silas Moshoela of Mafeking. We knew each other very well at college, having attended the same philosophy classes and played rugby together. I was ecstatic at this unplanned meeting, as was he. "But I had read you had skipped the country; what are you doing in Jo'burg?" he asked.

I said, "Hush, follow me into the bathroom." We locked ourselves inside the little bathroom closet, and he worked away at the iron handcuffs with his pocket knife. I briefly explained that I was escaping from the police, and that any talking would have to be done later, as soon as I was under any roof that might serve as a temporary haven. After about twenty minutes we got the handcuffs off my wrist. He suggested we go to his place in Sophiatown for the night. I quickly rejected the idea—the police would check out the places of my former political associates or those with whom I had gone to school. I suggested that he should think of any girl he might know working in the white suburbs of Johannesburg. This seemed plausible to him. He suggested a place in the exclusive white suburb of Lower Houghton where a friend, Vuyelwa Calata, worked as a maid. There would be no problem with her accomodating me since she was from a politically active family in the Cape and was quite aware of the problems there. Her father, Reverend Calata, was a leader of the ANC in the Cape.

Silas got a taxi, and in about forty-five minutes we were at Vuyelwa's work place. Fortunately we got there before the 9:00 curfew and so were not stopped to be checked in regard to night passes. In areas like Lower Houghton there are hardly any police driving around or walking the beat. Middle-class white South Africans do not want to be disturbed even by car noises like screeching brakes or blowing horns. Most of their cars are chauffeur-driven by blacks who have to be out of town by sundown, as soon as they have chauffeured the bosses home from their offices. We had made a good choice for my temporary home.

Vuyelwa received us warmly after being told by Silas that I was a "hot cake," a term used by politically minded Africans to mean those being pursued by the police for political reasons. After serving us with cold drinks at her maid's quarters in the back of the main house, she left us to go about her cleaning and cooking chores. She would be back at about 11:00, the normal time for house servants to retire in South Africa, when the bosses go to bed.

Before I narrated my story in detail, Silas went out to look for a shebeen. Within thirty minutes he was back with a full bottle of Commando brandy. He made sure he was off the streets before curfew. After downing two long drinks I felt relaxed and told him my story.

Vuyelwa loaned me her one-room quarters for as long as I needed. She slept in the adjoining room with a friend who worked for the nextdoor neighbors, only coming in occasionally to keep me company and bring me food during her break time.

Silas visited me after work every day for the duration of my stay. We planned my next move.

Vuyelwa left me with a powerful transistor radio, and I tuned in often to learn what was happening in the outside world; I was indoors all the time except for going to the bathroom. At 6:00 the very first morning after my arrival I heard an announcement in both English and Afrikaans: "All South African Police in the Witwatersrand area, alert! Bantu male, Bransby Jordan, name known by Bojana Vuyisile, five feet, four inches, chocolate brown, slight scar above the right eye, wearing brown three-piece suit, white shirt and navy blue tie, heading for either Cape Town or Transkei. Check all bus stations, railways or cars driven by Bantu. Call nearest police station. For civilians cooperating, reward promised." This alert message was replayed about four times every day. By the time Silas returned to visit me, he too had heard the message. Because of the description, he had brought with him some old clothes and tennis shoes, as well as an old work hat. I immediately changed.

During the first few days of my forced stay in the Johannesburg suburbs, Silas was working around the clock to devise some means of getting me out of the country as soon as possible. He had contacted some old college friends of ours, Drs. Frank Mdlalose and Andrew Moriosele, who had a joint surgical practice in Attridgeville, Pretoria. On the third evening of my stay, a white friend drove us to Pretoria to the Mdlalose home. We got there safely. All the road blocks where police were trying to stop me were concentrated on the roads to the south leading either to Cape Town of the Transkei.

I rested in Pretoria for a day and a half while we busily planned how best to skip out of the country. It was decided that Dr. Moriosele, or "Andries," as we used to call him at Fort Hare, would drive me towards Mafeking—west of Johannesburg and near the Botswana border. His home was in the Mafeking area and he could speak the Tswana language of the people in this area well. I believe he has since opened up a practice in the so-called independent homeland of Bophutatswana, and Frank Mdlalose is now operating in another so-called homeland of KwaZulu. Even if this information about their having helped an "escapee from justice" reaches the government of

South Africa, they'll be quite safe, since they are no longer South Africans but belong to independent, "foreign" states.

Dressed in rags, I entered Andrew's car as just another of his patients whom he was taking to Mafeking. Fortunately, I could speak some Tswana since I had lived in Botswana for a few months. We drove through to Mafeking without incident. He left me at the home of Dr. S.M. Molema, another medical practitioner. Dr. Molema was an old friend of my family, having been educated at Fort Hare in the twenties with my uncle A.C. His patients were from around the Mafeking area and also across the border of Botswana in Barolong Farms. I spent another good night at Dr. Molema's home reminiscing about "the good old days" of college. The following day he was going to drive one of his patients from the Mafeking hospital across the border to Botswana. This seemed to suit my purpose perfectly. At long last there was a clear, distinct possibility that I would again be out of the hot political soup of South Africa.

Early the following day he bandaged my head so very little of my face showed. We drove to the hospital to be joined by another, real patient. From the hospital we were on our way to Botswana. When we got to the border Dr. Molema simply showed his medical license and declared he was returning his patients to Barolong Farms. No border policeman could doubt that I was a real patient because of the heavy bandages. My face could hardly be recognized even if they had a photo of me in front of them. Also, Dr. Molema was known to cross the border with his patients to and from Botswana. In South Africa there is an average of one doctor to about forty thousand blacks, so even the crude conscience of the South African police does not allow them to question the credentials and credibility of accredited doctors.

Once again I crossed the Botswana border without incident. We drove an extra five miles across the border to the nearest railway station, where I was to resume my journey by train, this time in the then-Bechuanaland Protectorate. Dr. Molema dropped me at the station with enough money to buy some food and a ticket to Lobatsi. Free at last!

The train reached Lobatsi at about noon that day. I alighted and went to the phone booth to call my old associates of the

Bechuanaland People's Party, with whom I previously had worked. Brother Kgaboesele was soon at the station to take me to his house, where I had a welcome bath and changed back into a three-piece suit. The first thing I did was to call collect the office of the chief of the Special Branch of the police in Johannesburg, Colonel T. Spengler. No matter how relieved I was to have escaped from South Africa once again, I could not resist the opportunity to get back at the police chief and make him aware that he was not master over all blacks in the world.

When the operator answered, I said I was calling collect because I was stranded at some railway station near the border and wanted to surrender to the police. Without any hesitation Colonel Spengler picked up the phone and accepted the call. "Where are you, kaffir?" he asked agitatedly.

"Safe as the Bank of England, under the protection of Her Majesty the Queen in Bechuanaland Protectorate," I replied, laughing as I pictured his tremendous anger and agitation.

"You bloody bastard you!" he replied and hung up. That was the last I ever heard from a South African police official. And may it forever be my last conversation with the South African police as long as they are capable of destroying me and any black African without our having recourse to democratic, legal procedures and guarantees of human rights.

To the best of my knowledge, the incident of my escape has not been repeated in recent times. Much later, after I was out of Botswana, I heard that Colonel Spengler was strongly reprimanded—possibly demoted—because he had let a "big fish" escape. I can only say I am happy I was able to pull it off with the help of several sons and daughters of the soil of Azania—those wonderful ones committed to service, sacrifice and suffering. They served me, they sacrificed their time and resources and they mitigated my suffering. May we all serve South African people until freedom and justice ring out across that beautiful land.

Teaching in Botswana

My escape from South Africa at the Jan Smuts Airport was a sensation, especially in the liberal press in South Africa. The weekly liberal party newspaper, *Contact*, headlined it, "Sir Roy

Wellensky Reneges on British Constitution and Fails to Protect Refugee." Side by side with Wellensky's photo in the paper was my picture with this caption under it, "Over my dead body will South Africa ever catch me." I do not remember to whom or when I said that, but I probably did say it.

Lobatsi was the legislative capital of the self-governing Bechuanaland British Protectorate territory. So when the newspapers were read by the townsfolk and the legislators about a week after my arrival, I became a small-time celebrity. In 1962 Gaberone, the present capital of Botswana lying about twenty miles north of Lobatsi, had four small shops, a combined bar and liquor store, a police station with four policemen, and a railway station. There were less than one hundred residents in a two-mile radius. I believe there are now over fifteen thousand residents.

Robert Mugabe wrote to tell me that the matter of my deportation from Southern Rhodesia had been raised by a British member of Parliament, pointing out its irregularity since I had been a political refugee. In retrospect, I know now it was just as well that I took the law into my own hands when I eluded the police in South Africa. The whole episode of my being picked up in Salisbury had been illegal on the part of both the Rhodesian and the South African governments. Why should I have been the one to legalize it by standing trial and thus granting legitimacy to both the Rhodesian and South African attempts to imprison me?

The two African political parties in Botswana prior to and after independence were the Botswana Democratic Party, led by Seretse Khama, and the Botswana People's Party, led by Philip Matante, a gifted orator called "The Lion of Botswana." The People's Party was very friendly and supportive of South African refugees. Actually, it helped both the ANC and the PAC refugees though it officially supported the PAC.* While

---

*Matante is quoted as saying in 1964, "We [the BPP] say that Africa is the land of the Africans, from the Cape to Cairo, from Morocco to Malagasy. Does this suggest that we are racialists? We believe that we are all one race: the human race. We say to hell with multiracialism, because it seeks to entrench racialism in our country." Paul Namlyn, *The New Africans,* Drury House, London, 1967.

the South African newspapers* were still full of stories about my escape, Philip Matante decided to strike while the iron was still hot and regularize my stay there by getting me a job.

So Philip and I went to the Education Department in Lobatsi. As before, there were few schools, all fully staffed. The only vacancy at the time existed in Tsetsebe Primary School in the Tati District near Francistown. The vacancy called for a Standards I to IV teacher of all subjects (equivalent to grades one to four). I had been trained as a secondary and high school teacher. The Tsetsebe post would have to be the lowest I could possibly take, if I did. The Botswana authorities, who were almost all white, probably did not expect me to accept the appointment, but after what I had been through I was ready to accept anything. Besides, I loved teaching and would never have left it had it not been for the Bantu Education Act. My only problem with teaching grades one through four would be my ignorance of the fine points of the Tswana language. Knowing how resourceful I could be when necessary, I gladly accepted the position. I was going to teach every subject in all the classes except Tswana; arrangements were made with the principal that, while I taught a class in a subject that was not Tswana-speaking, another teacher could be teaching Tswana in one of mine. I was determined to make the best of things in Botswana this time.

What was so appealing to me about teaching in Botswana was that I was going to be paid according to my qualifications regardless of what class of level I taught. Besides, there was no discrimination in regard to salary scales for blacks versus whites as there had been in South Africa. The British government had just passed new higher salary scales for its High Commission Territories, which included Botswana. My starting salary here was going to be double what I received as a teacher in South Africa. What was more, the cost of living was much lower in Botswana than it was in South Africa.

---

*The only newspapers that were read in the whole country of Botswana were either South African, Rhodesian or English. There was no local paper in the whole country.

When I started teaching a few days after my Lobatsi interview, I was very happy because everybody, teachers and students, went out of their way to make me feel at home. The Tswana people are among the most hospitable of the African nations. They usually go out of their way to make a *moeng*, or stranger, feel very comfortable. True enough, I did not teach Tswana, and I did not have as much of a language difficulty as I had anticipated. Tsetsebe is in the northern part of Botswana, where the predominant language is Kalanga. Kalanga people live near the border of western Zimbabwe, which is Ndebele-speaking; hence, most of the Kalangans speak Ndebele. Xhosa belongs to the same root family, Nguni, as Ndebele, so communications with students and parents were hardly a problem.

After two months I was transferred from Tsetsebe to Francistown Higher Primary School, where I was to teach Standards V and VI. These were the highest classes one could teach at the primary school level. Francistown was another small town with a tennis court, two bars and a hospital. The railway lines from Cape Town and Johannesburg met and merged in Mafeking, then continued through Botswana, Zimbabwe and Zambia. Francistown was on this line running north through Botswana and was the biggest railway station in the country. Every Saturday morning at about 10:00 I was sure to be found at the railway station just in case there might be some face I might recognize from South Africa. Even if there were no such face, I would invariably find someone I could converse with either in my language or in English just to learn how things were at home. First hand, verbal information is always so much more reliable, meaningful and personal than that from a newspaper. It makes you feel part of what you are talking about—a belonging for which I yearned as an exile.

By 1963 Francistown had been designated by the Botswana government and by the International Defense and Aid Fund as a major refugee center for South Africans. The site where South African refugees were received became famous thoughout Africa and was known as the "White House" because it was painted white. At that time I had never heard of another famous "White House"—in Washington, D.C. Many political refugees whom I had known in Cape Town were temporarily housed at the White House in Botswana as they passed through Francistown. In fact, I made it a rule to set aside at least one-third of my monthly salary to help these exiles with food and clothing as the need arose. I have since met a few of those I helped in Botswana in these United States.

I once again became active in teacher affairs, becoming the secretary of the Tati region of the Bechuanaland Protectorate Teachers' Association. This was a purely professional organization and I accepted that I was not to meddle in Botswana's political affairs. My concern was to keep a job and prepare myself for revolution. The fact that Francistown had become a refuge for South Africans going abroad for either further education or military training did not go unnoticed by the South African government.

A Refugee Plane Is Set Ablaze

Refugees were housed at the White House according to their political affiliation: ANC or PAC. The respective leaders of these groups would send detailed resumes of the people concerned to the headquarters-in-exile in Dar es Salaam, Tanzania. Headquarters then sent instructions regarding the disposition of the refugees—either for military training, further academic education or any other practicality for the struggle ahead. Planes were usually sent to pick up the refugees from the Francistown Airstrip just about a mile outside of town. The planes were usually a donation from one or another of the independent African countries or chartered by the International Defense and Aid Fund.

In November 1963 a plane was sent from Ghana by Osagyefo* Dr. Kwame Nkrumah to airlift the PAC refugees. Some of us were helping the freedom fighters pack their belongings and others were already proceeding to the airstrip on foot to board the plane. Suddenly a bright blaze of fire lit the sky, followed by a cascade of smoke from the direction of the airstrip. We knew without hesitation the plane had been set on fire. Fortunately,

---

Osagyefo is a title meaning "The Redeemer."

no one was inside; even the pilots were in town having their supper. Realizing that it was meant to destroy them all, the exiles who were to have been on that flight exclaimed, "The gods of Africa just saved us from extinction." It was later learned that a timed device had been set to engulf the plane with fire as it took off; the device went off earlier than anticipated. Investigations also revealed that thirty minutes earlier a car with two white occupants and with a Transvaal-Johannesburg number plate had stopped for two minutes near the plane and then sped off towards the Rhodesian border about half an hour away. This must have been the work of agents of the South African government.

That particular group of freedom fighters did not leave Francistown until two weeks later. From then onwards all airplanes landing in Botswana to pick up freedom fighters were carefully guarded from the time they landed until they left the country. It became common knowledge that South African police agents were coming to Botswana in various disguises to monitor what the freedom fighters were doing, so political refugees did not stop too long in Botswana. The protection from the Botswana government was not adequate, as Botswana was itself a very new country still struggling to make ends meet. It would have been very easy for the sophisticated South African police to kidnap refugees and take them back to South Africa to face jail sentences. It has never really been possible to train freedom fighters in neighboring countries, especially Botswana, because of the proximity to South Africa and because of their economic dependence on South Africa. Hence, Botswana was primarily used as a transit spot.

I never had the intention of settling in Botswana because of its insecure position and exposure to South Africa. Although I did enjoy my work, teaching in the primary schools was never really satisfactory to me. Besides, I wanted to be further north, closer to where I would be going for military or intelligence training or for propaganda work. Naturally, none of those training areas could be in any of the southern African countries which were themselves not yet independent.

9

Zambia, Last Home in Africa

There were no universities in Northern Rhodesia. All the university graduates in that country had studied either in Europe or in South Africa. Since Fort Hare University was the only center of advanced learning for blacks in South Africa, it was the alma mater for a large percentage of educated southern Africans. During my time at the University there were never more than 250 students each year, so after years each of us became well known to everyone else. This was especially true with those of us who were politically minded and met in small discussion groups. This personal knowledge of our classmates and their political views later served those of us from South Africa in good stead. We would have some steadfast friends in southern and central Africa in times of need. In the early sixties, the saying "A friend in need is a friend indeed" was continuously tested for its practical application to South African exiles.

Northern Rhodesia was to be the first stop on my northward journey. The transition date from the British-held Northern Rhodesia to African-ruled Zambia was set for October 24. The old Federation of the Rhodesias and Nyasaland, established in 1953, had crumbled largely because of opposition by African majorities in Northern Rhodesia and Nyasaland; following its dissolution, Northern Rhodesia, Southern Rhodesia and Nyasaland had returned to their former status of self-governing colonies. By 1963 all three colonies were clamoring for independence. In Zambia the majority-supported United National Independence Party was led by Kenneth Kaunda. Among its fifteen top officials, at least six were Fort Hare classmates of mine.

By mid-1964 I started correspondence with my former college colleagues in Northern Rhodesia with a view to paving the way for finding a teaching position there by the end of the year. Northern Rhodesia was due to get its independence by October. With the hope of securing a position by the end of the year, I resigned my teaching job at the end of September. A week prior to Zambian independence I left Francistown for Maun, bordering on Namibia, where arrangements were to be made for me to cross over to Zambia via the Caprivi Strip.

I wanted both to be an eyewitness to the induction of my former colleagues into positions of responsibility in the newly independent government and to present myself and my credentials, since I knew my qualifications were very respectable for job placement in Zambia.* Many Zambian leaders had had their university education in South Africa and recognized that it was second to none by world standards; at least, this was certainly the case before the advent of Bantu Education.

How was I to get to Northern Rhodesia without passing through Southern Rhodesia? I was *persona non grata* in the latter country. I knew very well that both the South African and Southern Rhodesian authorities had never forgiven me for my escape. Almost two years later, I would still have to be very careful not to risk being ensnared again by the Rhodesian police. A wounded political lion usually becomes more vicious when it is gasping for breath. The racist, dictatorial regimes of South Africa and Southern Rhodesia were being challenged by uprisings engineered by the liberatory movements at home and by the condemnation of the outside world of their suppressive

---

*"At independence in Zambia there were only four African doctors, half a dozen African lawyers and one African engineer." *The New Africans*, written by fifty correspondents of the Reuters News Agency, Paul Hamlyn Ltd., London, 1967.

policies. The very fact that Northern Rhodesia was soon to be free and independent probably caused some sleepless nights for the authorities in the still-oppressed countries of the south. Both countries had tightened their belts of oppression with more and more detailed statutes and enlarged police battalions and armaments. It would have been the height of folly on my part to even consider risking travel through Southern Rhodesia.

With these concerns foremost in my mind, I left Francistown by bus for Maun, the last outpost before the Botswana-Namibia border to the northwest. The roads were very bad and it took us two days and nights of steady traveling to cover approximately 260 miles. I believe that journey now can be completed in about ten hours since the roads have been tarred. I would be picked up from Maun and would cross the Zambezi River in the Caprivi Strip (part of Namibia) at Kazungula. After a few days in Maun I joined two other South Africans, Martha Nkula and her son Dedanizizwe, en route to Zambia. We were picked up by an official UNIP truck arriving from Livingstone; this had been organized by Keke Nkula, Martha's husband, who worked at the Pan-Africanist Congress office in Dar es Salaam. He had also arranged for the clearance of his family's travel documents into Zambia. No such travel documents could be arranged for me. I was to receive papers as soon after independence as was humanly possible; I had been warned to stay in Botswana until then. But I wanted to take advantage of the first ride out and I was enthusiastic about the possibility of securing a secondary school teaching assignment, so I traveled with the Nkulas as far as Kazungula but devised an alternate plan to enter Zambia.

The outpost city of Kazungula is located at a strategic point at the eastern end of the Caprivi Strip where four African countries meet: Namibia, Botswana, Zambia and Zimbabwe. Part of Kazungula lies in Botswana and part in Zambia. At the crossing point, Kazungula Bridge, several South African refugees were awaiting clearance by the Northern Rhodesian Immigration officials. Representatives from both South African liberatory movements were there to help out in any dispute, ready to sit down with the officials and go through any doubtful political credentials. This could take hours. The two Pan-Africanist Congress representatives screening the exiles were Ngqondi

Masimini and Bekabantu Ngcobo. Both knew me well and would not have hesitated to vouch 100 percent for me. The problem was my badly shaken faith in the Rhodesian police after what had happened to me in Salisbury. Yet at the same time I was determined to somehow cross the Zambezi into Zambia. I decided not to attempt to cross the border at the Kazungula Bridge as it might have meant running the risk of being spotted by South African special agents planted at all the border crossings in southern African countries. Especially in Kazungula there would be South African officials from South-West Africa (Namibia) since that country was and still is held in bondage by the Republic of South Africa.*

As I thought of the route by which migrant mine laborers had been moved across borders in southern Africa, a plan came to mind. Ever since anyone can remember, over half of South Africa's mine workers had come from outside the borders of South Africa. Many of them came from the so-called High Commission Territories of Basotoland (Lesotho), Bechuanaland (Botswana) and Swaziland. Others came from the so-called Portuguese East and West Africa (Mozambique and Angola, respectively), and still more came from the two Rhodesias and

---

*From the end of World War I until the end of World War II, the South African government administered the former German colony of South-West Africa under a mandate from the old League of Nations. When the United Nations came into being, its Charter provided that all previously mandated, dependent territories come under its supervision. South Africa moved to incorporate the land within its own borders regardless of UN protests. Each year the UN has passed resolutions condemning South Africa for its failure to live up to the terms of the Charter, but they have come to nothing. During the 1960s, a political group took shape in South-West Africa calling itself the South-West African People's Organization, or SWAPO. SWAPO's aim is to gain independence for the territory from South Africa. In 1966 the UN demanded that South Africa terminate its rule over South-West Africa, but South Africa refused, saying it had the military power to back it up. South Africa set up a constitution for the territory with the intention of assuring continued white control. The UN re-named the territory Namibia and set up a Namibia Council, but this didn't affect the South African government at all. In 1978 South Africa placed over eighteen thousand troops in the territory and promoted the Democratic Turnhalle Alliance, a multi-racial coalition of conservative parties dominated by white leadership. These are still the conditions in South Africa, with the UN and SWAPO still objecting.

Nyasaland. The South African Company (actually the Anglo-American Company) headed by Harry F. Oppenheimer contracted a labor agency called WENELA to recruit in all these territories. WENELA had a large number of trucks which helped workers reach South Africa by transporting them from areas far removed from the railroads to the nearest railway stations and then by rail to South Africa.

The nearest railway station for northeast Botswana was in Livingstone, Northern Rhodesia. Twice a week a WENELA truck came down to Kazungula, Botswana, to pick up migrant mine workers and take them to Livingstone, where they could then board the train for South Africa. Fortunately the day after our arrival at Kazungula was a Wednesday, the regularly scheduled day to transport miners to Livingstone. The WENELA driver who held the list of workers to be picked up—a list approved by the Northern Rhodesian government for transit—happened to be keenly politically conscious and spoke the Ndebele language. I took him aside and explained my predicament: no legal papers to cross over to Livingstone. I also assured him that once over on Zambian soil I would be no trouble; rather I'd be very much on my own negotiating with top UNIP officials. The WENELA driver only required that I change my name to a common Tswana one which he put among the list of twenty-seven he was supposed to pick up.

We all sat in the back of the truck—no seats—the typical way black laborers were transported. When we crossed over the border, the driver just handed over the list of workers to the border authorities. The immigration authorities never really worried about checking any of the details in regard to the truck's passengers. They always took the driver's word that everything was in order. Once we reached Livingstone, I thanked the driver by putting the equivalent of five dollars in the palm of his right hand. From then onwards I was on my own.

The other South African refugees, who had crossed legally, had arrived in Livingstone before me and were in the immigration offices being processed. I had no intention of going near where Rhodesian law enforcers would be located. Rather, I took my things off the WENELA truck and went to the home of my South African friend, Bolofo, who was a teacher in Livingstone.

The Independent Country of Zambia

A day later I was on a train to the capital, Lusaka, where I was met by friends from the PAC House in Kamwala. I lived in the township of Kamwala with the other freedom fighters from South Africa until freedom day for Northern Rhodesia arrived. It almost seemed like freedom day for me, too, yet in the back of my mind was always the thought, "How I wish this were freedom for my people in South Africa." On Friday, October 24, 1964, Northern Rhodesia became the independent Republic of Zambia. I attended the independence celebrations at the Matero Stadium with thousands—it seemed like millions—of other Africans from all over the continent.

During the week-long celebration of independence, I was walking down Cairo Road in Lusaka one day when I heard a man calling to me from the other side of the street. It was none other than Pat Murphy, who was once a teacher of mine at Fort Hare. In 1951 he had been deported by the South African government for inviting African students to his house for drinks, parties and discussions. In Lusaka in 1964 he was representing the U.S. State Department during the Zambian independence celebrations. We went to the Ridgeway Hotel to talk of the good and the bad old days at Fort Hare; this went on until the early hours of the morning. Pat was now the executive director of the African American Institute, which granted scholarships, especially to South African students, to continue their education in the United States. He gave me a note to take to the U.S. Embassy, where I was to apply for a scholarship to do graduate work in the United States. I filled out all the application forms and was told I would have to wait unti further word from the Embassy.

Prior to Independence Day I had met several of my former Fort Hare colleagues who were to be sworn into Zambian governmental positions on the day of independence: Sikota Wina, to be Minister of Local Government and Housing; Elijah Mudenda, to be Minister of Agriculture; and Mupange Monakatwe, to be Minister of Education. The Friday evening celebration was followed by numerous festivities over the weekend, including sports and dances. Amidst all this excitement, all I could think of was my appointment with the Secretary of Education on Monday morning. On that morning I was hired as a history teacher at Chiwala Secondary School in Ndola, effective as soon as I could get there. I reported to the senior history class on Tuesday at 9:00 a.m. I was delighted with the thought of being back in the classroom to teach and take care of the young minds of Africans in a free and independent Zambia. Final examinations were taking place, and as the school term ended in November, I did not do much actual teaching; instead, I was assigned to invigilate, or proctor, examinations. The important thing to me was that I was employed and happily settled—far from South Africa in a level of teaching for which I was well qualified.

During the few months I had in Ndola, I learned some important things about this sprawling, land-locked country called Zambia, which is as large as three European countries or four of the western United States. Like South Africa, Zambia has rich mines, mainly copper, which is why the ninety-mile corridor in the middle of the country, where Ndola is located, is named the Copperbelt Province. This is one of the principal reasons Zambia at the time of independence was one of the richest countries in southern Africa, second only to South Africa. Unfortunately, the seven copper mines in Zambia were largely controlled and operated by a white minority whose interests did not always coincide with aiding the majority African population. The major cities in the Copperbelt—Ndola, Kitwe and Mufulira—were garden spots created around luxurious homes, golf courses and country clubs for whites only. President Kaunda had to contend with many such internal problems. For me, the struggle lay in South Africa; in Zambia I was there to contribute to the educational process, not politics.

At the beginning of the new school year, early in 1965, I was transferred to teach in Mongu High School in southwestern Zambia among the Lozi-speaking people. This was an interesting contrast to Ndola. I very much enjoyed teaching at Mongu, especially because the Lozi language is very similar to Sotho and Tswana, languages which I had grown used to speak-

197

ing in Botswana. Besides the people were kind and rural, which reminded me of the Transkei. How I remember their respect and manners, especially towards strangers and elderly people! Men, women, children—all would kneel and clap their hands twice in greeting to welcome a guest, no matter who it was.

The Kuomboka ceremony was a social event that impressed me very much soon after my arrival in Mongu. This is the occasion when the Litunga, king of the BaLozi, and his people move with great joyousness and ceremony to the winter capital at Limulunga near Mongu. The move is necessary because the site of the summer capital lies in the center of the Barotse Plain, which becomes submerged by the swollen Zambezi River. For centuries the people have believed that this seasonal flooding dates back to the time of the Great Flood, known as *Meya-a-Luangwanga*, "The Water That Drowned Everything." This evacuation to the higher ground has always been marked by rich pageantry and great festivities. At the time the Litunga decides to leave, usually in March, or February if the rains are early and heavy, drums send out the signal for the move, directing the people to pack all their household goods in canoes for an imminent departure.

The flotilla of canoes is headed by the Litunga's royal barge, the Nalikwanda, ninety feet long and fifteen feet in beam, with its thirty paddlers in colorful array. The Litunga's wife, the Moyo, has her own royal barge, which is followed by an armada of assorted craft. The chanting of African music accompanies this flotilla as it glides over the waters. Crossing the flooded plain to the new capital takes about five or six hours. Near the new capital a crowd awaits. As the paramount chief and royal barge are sighted, a tremendous roar goes up from the crowd. Then people perform the royal greeting dance, the Kushowelela, to commemorate the safe arrival of the fleet. For days and nights there is much excitement and celebration, with traditional dancing, singing, drumming, xylophone playing, eating and drinking.*

---

*The return journey after the flood waters have receded is not commemorated with any special celebration. It is the crossing from the danger of the flooding waters to the safety of the high grounds and temporary quarters that gives the Kuomboka its great significance.

As 1965 was Zambia's first year of independence, President Kaunda and almost his entire cabinet made it a most meaningful occasion by going to Leauli for the ceremony. The importance of the event was such that even in colonial days governors had often attended. During the ceremony in 1965, it was my great pleasure and privilege to arrange a short welcome party for almost all of the cabinet ministers, especially those who indulged in alcoholic beverages. President Kaunda arrived at my house but remained seated outside the door after he looked in and saw everyone imbibing. He was looking for Justin Chimba, his Minister of Commerce and Industry. Two of the cabinet ministers and their wives were living with me during the week of the ceremony. This was possible in Mongu, since I lived in a huge government house with three bedrooms and a very large living room. These were houses that, prior to independence, had been the preserve of white expatriate families, particularly from England.

The first semester or school quarter ended towards the end of March each year. It so happened that a history teacher was urgently needed at Chipepo Secondary School in southeast Zambia, adjacent to the Kariba Dam. When a transfer of teachers had to be made, the policy was "Last hired, first transferred." This was quite logical and understandable to most of us. Students should not be deprived of the services of a teacher to whom they have become accustomed, nor should a teacher be disturbed when he or she has already established a rapport with the students. Also the teacher's family has probably become somewhat rooted in the area. I surely was last hired, since I had only been there three months. I was not with a family, I fully understood the Ministry of Education's policies and, besides, this was a great way to see and learn about different parts of the country. So, when the second school term opened in April, I was on my way to a new School.

When I passed through the capital, Lusaka, to pick up the transfer papers en route to Chipepo, I checked in at the PAC on Cairo Road as I had often done whenever I happened to be in town. I was very keen to hear about any new developments in South Africa. I found that all was still quiet on the apartheid front, with people's emotional attitudes as bitter as ever. The only good news from the PAC office was that the United States Embassy had called to say I had been selected to do graduate work in the United States. The message also stated that I should get in touch with the Embassy to make arrangements to leave for the United States by the beginning of their next school term in September. I went to the U.S. Embassy the following day to indicate that I would be ready to leave for the States during the winter school vacation, which falls from June to July in Zambia. This would also provide me the opportunity to serve one term in my teaching job at Chipepo and give the required notice of intention to resign in June.

I arrived at Chipepo the following day and started class duties the next. I taught history and English in four of the classes in Forms I and II. Once again I enjoyed my work. African students are such a pleasure to work with because of their respect for their elders. I never had one-hundredth of the disciplinary problems while I taught all over southern Africa that I had during the time I taught school in the cities of the United States. It is a matter of two different cultures and their commitments to varying degrees of respect, obedience and permissiveness.

The most striking scenes around Chipepo were the Kariba Dam, about two miles from the school, and the Victoria Falls. The Dam was built in 1955 for about ninety million pounds, a huge, prestigious project of the Federation of Rhodesia and Nyasaland. It was meant to tame the Zambezi and create the biggest man-made lake, at the time, in the world. The federal prime minister, Lord Malvern, told the Assembly, "Its size and all that sort of thing makes such a popular appeal and it will be an excellent advertisement for the whole federal area." The Federation of the Rhodesias and Nyasaland, which was formed by settlers against the will of the African people, did not last more than a decade, but the Kariba Dam is still there and is now primarily used as a hydroelectric plant. The lake behind the dam offers fishing and sailing pleasures. Near Chipepo, parts of the shoreline have been declared a wildlife reserve. Some weekends when I did not go either to Lusaka or Livingstone, I used to watch wildlife roaming their sanctuary along the shore.

About forty miles to the south of Chipepo, near the city of Livingstone, can be found the greatest sheet of flowing water in the world—the Victoria Falls on the Zambezi River. The Victoria Falls are twice as high as Niagara Falls in the United States and have a width of about one mile. When the river is swollen with flood waters from the summer rains, about 75 million gallons are spilled every minute into the 1,860-yard fissure. As the water crashes down, it sends up fine columns of spray which appear to mingle with the clouds and can be seen twelve miles away. This is why Africans call the falls *Musi-oa-tunya,* meaning "The Smoke That Thunders." This is the largest curtain of falling water in the world and easily the greatest and most spectacular sight in Africa. Even today, apart from the single-span arch bridge over the gorge dividing Zambia and Zimbabwe, tourists still see the falls as David Livingstone saw them when he is reported to have said, "Scenes so lively must be gazed upon by angels in their flight." According to the people who live in the area around the falls, down below in the deep chasm is the home of the rainbow, where the great gods of Africa sleep. There is also a common tale of a pot of gold buried where the rainbow ends; this is surely nature's gift of this vision of beauty.

This is a brief picture of the Zambia I knew during my nine months in the country, an independent and free Zambia, a beautiful Zambia of the Kuomboka ceremony near Mongu, and a heavenly Zambia of the Musi-oa-tunya near Chipepo. Why would I want to leave Africa, especially independent Zambia, which had given me a teaching job, a pleasant residence, glorious nature and, above all, freedom itself? What more could anyone from South Africa want? The answer for me was that I still wanted freedom in my own land.

The school term had come to an end with the winter holidays, and I had made up my mind to leave by mid-August. The U.S. Embassy had arranged a visa, travel documents and an air ticket for me. I would miss Africa. I would miss home. Why was I leaving? Why the United States?

> *There may I rest from pursuit.*
> *There may I find freedom and justice.*
> *There may I speak to people who will help.*
> *Let me now journey to this new land.*

The United States of America

From early childhood, my father and his friends had always emphasized that we Africans had other African relatives who centuries ago had left against their will for America and had been forced to work for the white man. This early childhood education was further enlarged by my history studies, which explained how African-Americans had been tranported to the United States as slaves while everybody else traveled in a *Mayflower*. Some of my ancestors were in the United States by 1619, maybe even arriving in the shipload that disembarked in Jamestown, Virginia. This is probably before the ancestors of the Kennedys, the Johnsons, the Nixons, the Carters or the Reagans arrived on America's shores. One thing is certain: Africans did not come to America to exploit or enslave others. They came to work and to make America what it is today. America was built on the blood, sweat and tears of African men and women who were forcibly brought to the North American continent during the sixteenth, seventeenth and eighteenth centuries. Their bones are buried in the soil of the cotton and the tobacco fields of the agricultural South, beneath the skyscrapers which house the financial institutions of America, and under the factories which are the way of life for many of those who live there.

I came to the United States to study and further my career in education, but within me was a great desire to live with and learn about my brothers and sisters of African descent who had long since left Africa. I felt I would not be considered a complete foreigner. Also I wanted to reach out, to educate the majority of Americans of European ancestry about the plight of the people of South Africa. Surely the American people did not know about the oppressive apartheid system under which my people were forced to live. I knew how much trade the United States was doing with South Africa due to the cheap black labor there, productivity based on the agonies of my people locked in a caste system. I knew the financial support that the multinationals were giving to the racist South African regime to keep generation after generation of blacks downtrodden in the land of their birth. Also, American companies are helping to exhaust the natural resources of the land before Africans could benefit from them. Even the land which South Africans need to grow food for their very survival is being taken from them by a government that allows them no representation. These companies, through their economic and political ties to the racist South African government, have been profiting immeasurably from the misery of the black people of South Africa.*

How could a "great" country like the United States have dealings with a dictatorship like South Africa? I knew that the United States government had favored and signed many, many declarations of human rights. The United Nations, with its charter dedicated to freedom and well-being for all the peoples of the world, had been placed in that country. Surely the American people did not know what I knew about South Africa.

I had even read and been told in my American history courses how the country of the United States had come into being—how black and white people together had fought the powerful British Empire in their own revolution to achieve "life, liberty and the pursuit of happiness." I believed I could, through the education system, influence these sons and daughters of the American Revolution to aid in the cause of liberation for South Africans. "Now help us!" I wanted to cry. I felt confident that the United States would be on the side of righteousness, of human rights and justice for all.

In August 1965, with great hopes and expectations and with some sadness to be leaving Africa, my Africa, I boarded the BOAC flight in Lusaka, Zambia, bound for the United States of America.

***

Postscript, Summer 1986: After all these years in the United States, I yearn for Africa, especially its southernmost tip. So much has happened politically since my departure and so much more is happening at this moment. After scrupulously monitor-

---

*As of this writing there are roughly five hundred American companies doing business in South Africa, with a total investment of over $14.6 billion in that country.

ing and analyzing events at home, there is no doubt in my mind that, come rain or shine, freedom for its indigenous people is around the corner. The land of Azania is now being liberated from the usurpers by its rightful owners. Izwe Lelethu!

People have since adopted methods best suited to maximize their talents and skills in order to topple, once and for all, the racist system and replace it with a truly democratic society. Throughout South Africa, it is a matter of life and death on the part of the people to restore sanity to a system of unbridled brutality and barbarism as enacted by the white racist government. In the 1960s the people acquired psychological weapons to challenge the oppressor openly; in the 1970s they lost their fear of the oppressor's guns; in the 1980s they are seizing with clenched fists what they could not get by offering an open hand.

The people have made up their minds to stick it out and to fight on. In doing so, they contemptuously disregard the heavy odds and rising toll in deaths, detentions, prison murders and graveside massacres. Once the bull had been taken by the horns, the people resolved not to slacken their grip—to make sure *we will be heard*.

FOOTNOTES

[1]*Report of the Inter-Departmental Committee on Native Education,* 1935-1936.

[2]Denis Herbstein, *White Man We Want to Talk to You,* London, 1979.

[3]Denis Herbstein.

[4]Denis Herbstein.

[5]House of Assembly Debates, September 17, 1953.

[6]Edgar H. Brookes, *Apartheid: A Documentary Study of Modern South Africa,* New York, 1969.

[7]House of Assembly Debates, June 7, 1959.

[8]I.B. Tabata, *Education for Barbarism,* London, 1960.

[9]*Speeches of Mangaliso Sobukwe from 1949 to 1959 and Other Documents of the Pan-Africanist Congress of Azania,* PAC Observer Mission to the United Nations, New York.

[10]*Speeches of Mangaliso Sobukwe.*

[11]I.B. Tabata.

[12]I.B. Tabata.

[13]Govan Mbeki, *South Africa: The Peasants' Revolt,* Middlesex, 1964.

[14]Edgar Brookes.

[15]I.B. Tabata.

[16]Trevor Huddleston CR, *Naught for Your Comfort,* New York, 1956.

[17]*National Geographic,* April 1931.

[18]See "South Africa Is Planning to Uproot a Tribe of 50,000," *The New York Times,* December 6, 1979.

[19]*Speeches of Mangaliso Sobukwe.*

[20]*Speeches of Mangaliso Sobukwe.*